ID0984485

A MASTER OF
SURPRISE

A MASTER OF
SURPRISE

Mark Interpreted

Donald H. Juel

FORTRESS PRESS   *Minneapolis*

A MASTER OF SURPRISE
Mark Interpreted

Scripture quotations unless otherwise noted are from the New Revised Standard Version Bible, copyright © 1989 by the Division of Christian Education of the National Council of the Churches of Christ in the United States.

Portions of Chapter 3 are based in part on the author's essay "The Baptism of Jesus (Mark 1:9-11)," which appears in Arland J. Hultgren, Donald H. Juel, and Jack D. Kingsbury, *All Things New* Supplement Series 1 (1992): 119–26. Copyright © *Word and World* 1992 and reprinted with permission.

Cover design: Cindy Cobb Olson

Library of Congress Cataloging-in-Publication Data

Juel, Donald.
    A master of surprise : Mark interpreted / Donald H. Juel.
      p.   cm.
    Includes bibliographical references and index.
    ISBN 0-8006-2594-3 (alk. paper) :
    1. Bible. N.T. Mark—Criticism, interpretation, etc.   I. Title.
BS2585.2.J84   1994
226.3'06—dc20   94-6132
                                         CIP

The paper used in this publication meets the minimum requirements of American National Standard for Information Sciences—Permanence of Paper for Printed Library Materials, ANSI Z329.48-1984. ∞™

Manufactured in the U.S.A.   AF 1-2594

98   97   96   95   94   1   2   3   4   5   6   7   8   9   10

Contents

Preface

My own engagement with the Gospel of Mark began with a seminary course from Roy Harrisville. He had become interested in redaction criticism and convinced several of us to translate Willi Marxsen's *Der Evangelist Markus* as our class project.[1] Marxsen's approach did not attract me—the redaction critical enterprise seemed to me largely undoable, particularly with regard to Mark's Gospel, and the arguments about tradition and redaction unconvincing—but I was captivated by Mark. My graduate work on the passion narrative with Nils Dahl only whetted my appetite for further study.[2]

After more than twenty years of work on the Gospel, I have written a commentary on Mark[3] and produced this book, which gathers up my reflections, a few of which have been published. The chapters have various histories: Some were written as long as ten years ago; others were written more recently for this volume. The chapters ideally should have been published with the commentary, but they were not all written. In retrospect the pause has been salutary. I have changed my mind about some things and benefited from new ideas since 1990. I do feel obliged to offer one apology. Robert Fowler's *Let the Reader Understand*[4] is one

1. Willi Marxsen, *Mark the Evangelist: Studies on the Redaction History of the Gospel*, trans. Roy A. Harrisville (Nashville: Abingdon, 1969).

2. Donald Juel, *Messiah and Temple: The Trial of Jesus in the Gospel of Mark*, SBLDS 31 (Missoula, Mont.: Scholars Press, 1977).

3. Juel, *Mark*, Augsburg Commentary on the New Testament Series (Minneapolis: Augsburg Books, 1990).

4. Robert Fowler, *Let the Reader Understand: Reader Response Criticism and the Gospel of Mark* (Minneapolis: Fortress Press, 1991).

of the most interesting books that I have read in the last years, and
were I to take his work into account, I would have to make some
substantial revisions to my categories.

Many persons deserve public appreciation. Foremost are my students,
whose critical questions and creative ideas have forever shaped my reading of the New Testament. I owe a debt of gratitude likewise to my
colleagues, particularly to Patrick Keifert and Mary Knutsen, who have
gradually helped me to understand what I am about as an interpreter
and whose unselfish gift of time and energy has provided continual
stimulation and encouragement. Kyle Halverson deserves special thanks
for his careful reading of the manuscript, and David Knox-Juel for
preparing the indices. I wish finally to thank Luther Northwestern
Seminary for the sabbatical support that provided time to work and the
Fortress Press staff, especially Timothy Staveteig, acquisitions editor,
and Julie Odland, production editor, for their efforts in getting the
book into print. As always, my deepest appreciation goes to my wife,
Lynda, whose patience, support, and encouragement have been more
important than she can know.

Part One

The Sense of Something Compelling

A Rhetorical Strategy for Reading Mark's Gospel

I confess that I have been captivated by the work we know as the Gospel according to Mark. I am not alone. Mark's Gospel has attracted at least as many admirers within my generation as Matthew's, Luke's, or John's. That would surely have surprised an Augustine, or a Luther, or Calvin. The absence of references to Mark among the great thinkers of the church bears eloquent testimony to a massive indifference. Few read Mark. Augustine apparently convinced many that, as Matthew's epitome, Mark's Gospel was an interesting but pale imitation of the real thing. Matthew's Gospel was the church's book; John's was the favorite of the more spiritually inclined.

Many reasons can be offered for this indifference, some of which I explore in chapter 2. The barbarous Greek and the palpable absence of style were reason enough for some to shun the shortest of the Gospels. Piecemeal reading that came to dominate liturgical practice meant that little was invested in the integrity of any of the Gospels. And because the version of Mark that has been perpetuated in standard Bible versions from the Vulgate to the Authorized Version concludes in chapter 16 with twenty verses that tie up all loose ends, there is little to engage the imagination of readers. The discovery that the best manuscripts conclude with, "For they were afraid" (16:8), surely provided one of the little shocks that awakened readers to the surprises that awaited a sympathetic audience.

My work offers an interpretation of the Gospel from a particular perspective. To a large degree, my struggle has been to clarify that perspective so as to understand in what sense my work is related to and different from current alternatives. The enterprise is worth some effort because publications on Mark continue to dominate Gospel literature even though presently no consensus exists on Mark as, say, on the Gospel of John. Tendencies among interpreters can be observed. Literary study has become a dominant feature of current studies, with a new set of standard work by scholars, such as Seymour Chatman, Wayne Booth, and George Kennedy. Sociology has left its mark on Markan scholarship through Howard Kee and others. Rhetorical criticism has provided promising directions, for example, by means of Vernon Robbins and John Donahue. Fewer scholars are interested in the compositional history of the Gospel (redaction criticism in the narrow sense)—although such studies continue to appear. Markan scholarship still seems fragmented, however, despite the efforts of Norman Perrin and others within the professional societies to draw things together.

Indeed, four observations about the present situation may help establish an interpretive context.

1. Methodology continues to dominate scholarship. Books invest a large portion of the opening chapters to spell out new methods.[1] Yet little consensus has emerged about the uses to which Mark can be put or the goals of research. Among current alternatives, I am attracted to scholarship produced by Fowler and Kermode who are principally interested in an engagement with the narrative. My colleague, Patrick Keifert, has suggested a series of models by which interpretation can be categorized.[2] The wide range of interpretive approaches, from the purely historical to the completely ahistorical, focus on legitimate aspects of biblical literature. Keifert sorts out interpretive strategies from form criticism, redaction criticism, and literary criticism to structuralism, indicating the degree to which a particular approach is historical (seeking something behind the text) or linguistic (seeking something within the story-world). He is interested not simply to profile interpretive strategies but to press the question about the goal of engagement with the Bible, What is the Bible good for? Of his categories, "story reader" seems to me the most engaging and promising approach. As a reader of the Bible, I am not interested principally in the history behind the Gospel, although historical considerations are important; I am not principally interested

1. Examples of recent books with concentration on methodology include Mary Ann Tolbert, *Sowing the Gospel: Mark's World in Literary-Historical Perspective* (Minneapolis: Fortress Press, 1989), and Fowler, *Let the Reader.*

2. See Patrick Keifert, "Mind-Reader and Maestro: Models for Understanding Biblical Interpreters," *Word and World* 1 (1981): 153–68, and his "Meaning and Reference: The Interpretation of Verisimilitude in the Gospel according to Mark" (Ph.D. diss., University of Chicago, 1982).

in the communities behind the Gospel nor the intention of the author; and I agree with Paul Ricoeur and George Steiner that the various decodings of the text—whether by Marxists or structuralists—may be a preamble to interpretation, but are not its end. I am principally interested in an engagement with the story—with the "world in front of the text"—which may benefit from the various approaches, but is a distinct enterprise.

2. Scholarship over the last half century has been dominated by historical methodologies. One of the troubling aspects of such scholarship is its ability to create an audience interested only in what the scriptural material meant to someone else at another time and place. There are perhaps many factors that have contributed to the present situation. One is the location of biblical scholarship at colleges and universities where rules of the interpretive game seem to demand descriptive scholarship. The Bible is studied as an ancient artifact. The approach has made possible ecumenical study at a grand level, but the cost has been great. A gulf between Scripture and present readership has been created that is difficult to bridge. Students are taught that what the Bible means is what it meant. Once firmly located at a different time and place, biblical works are difficult to drag into the present. We are left with what a colleague termed the "spent voice of the text." Meaning is all used up on someone else. While more literary and rhetorical approaches have begun to alter the scene, biblical scholarship at the professional level remains largely descriptive.

The situation cannot be traced solely to the shift to university from ecclesial settings for study of the Bible. Historical scholarship within the church has had a long and noble history. Among its goals was to free the Bible from the tyranny of church dogma and to provide a stable foundation on which to build a more adequate and engaging reading of the Bible in the present. So-called substantial historical facts are hard to come by, however, and the past turns out to have a future we cannot control or predict. Few would have imagined at the turn of the century how dramatically George Foote Moore's classic work on Judaism would have to be revised within decades of its publication; representatives of the Biblical Theology movement would have had difficulty believing that the distinction between Hebrew and Greek, so central to their construct, could be called into question so quickly and completely. The enormous investment in historical study among biblical scholars has not succeeded in providing stability for interpreters. It is not even clear at the moment what will become of the theories about the Qumran Scrolls, which have become foundational for the present generation of interpreters. The last decades of historical scholarship seem a conspiracy against historicist assumptions about studying history.

Further, the study of history has a way of becoming an end in itself. In a sophisticated study of the parables in Mark, Mary Ann Tolbert makes a distinction between "authorial audience" and "contemporary audience." Her interest, she insists, is in the former and not the latter:

> If the Gospels are to continue as *living* texts, then modern readers must always be able to interpret them in the light of current theological reflection and discourse. The terms used to describe the new or unique character of the Gospels by scholars (i.e., kerygma, parable) are not "new" or "unique" to their own peers and thus are suitable designations for the shared generic expectations of current readers. Those scholars who have explored the Greco-Roman and Jewish milieu of the Gospels, on the other hand, while still contemporary interpreters themselves, are attempting to read the Gospels in the light of their *authorial audience*. Thus the division between the two major streams of research on the gospel genre may be understood as attempts to clarify the reading process in terms of quite different, but equally legitimate, audiences, the contemporary and the authorial.[3]

The issue is how these two "attempts to clarify the reading process" are related. I can imagine no sound reason for interest in study of the Bible if it does not provide for more lively engagement with the material. Creating an audience interested only in the "authorial audience" is a rhetorical strategy that will not succeed in facilitating engagement. Readers will be left at a distance. And that is precisely the result of biblical scholarship among the enlightened. Students are not opened to the material, but are distanced from it; they are not helped to become better interpreters, but are often paralyzed by the sheer weight of scholarship. If scholarship does not produce better readers, then it is not only a waste of time but also genuinely harmful, and there are good reasons for churches to regard such scholarship with suspicion.

Occasionally this reminder can prove healthy: One need know nothing about the ancient world to read the Bible. People have been reading the Scriptures for centuries without the benefit of scholarly preparation. There are nevertheless good reasons to study the Bible. We do so to enlarge our imaginations. We are all limited by culture, language, gender, and class. Our relationship to others must respect their otherness. We need to be prepared to learn things we did not know, to be surprised in a variety of ways. We study the Bible and its historical and linguistic environment so as to make reading a richer experience or to adjudicate our serious differences of opinion.

3. Tolbert, *Sowing,* 57.

We cannot abandon historical studies any more than we can abandon our native tongue, especially because the Bible is located in particular times and cultures and because it makes referential claims about people and places. We can, however, learn where to locate historical study in the interpretive enterprise.

3. The burgeoning of more appreciative approaches to the New Testament has been salutary. Awareness of the linguistic character of the Gospels has opened new horizons. Students who spend the two hours watching and listening to David Rhoads's presentation of Mark or who participate in one of Tom Boomershine's seminars discover that the Gospels are never the same. They can be read and heard not simply as a collection of discrete snippets but as stories that are interesting, engaging, and intriguing. Mark's Gospel in particular has enjoyed a hearing it has rarely, if ever, received in the history of the church.

Such approaches to the Gospel locate the "problem" of history in a different place. If the goal of reading and hearing is engagement with the story, then historical study will have a subsidiary role to play. It cannot, however, be ignored. While all literature is fictive, fictionality needs to be measured by degrees. The New Testament makes referential claims that cannot be overlooked. The experience of reading a parable, for example, is quite different from hearing the account of Jesus' trial and death. One is not moved to ask about the name of the Samaritan who helped the injured man or the precise location of the farm where a sower scattered seed. It is a different matter, however, to read about how Jesus was executed at a place called Golgotha, during the term of Pontius Pilate, between nine in the morning and six at night on the feast of Passover, the eve of the Sabbath. The details cry for attention. One might well conclude that such details arose from the imagination of those who told the story of Jesus, but such a conclusion would have an important bearing on evaluating the truth claims of the respective accounts.

I recall listening to a learned address in the early 1970s on Mark's account of Jesus' death. The audience was a group of high school literature teachers who were studying ways of teaching the Bible in high school English classes. The lecturer gave a marvelous reading of the passion story as a typical account of a promising young man who took on the establishment, only to be crushed in the end. He drew on the recent experience of the audience, and much of his argument was compelling. It occurred to me afterward, however, that his reading was purchased at the expense of all the particulars in the story. Mark's Gospel does not claim to be typical, however much the author employs conventions, but purports to be about Jesus Christ, the Son of God, the crucified and risen King of the Jews. To make his argument, the lecturer had to ignore all of the royal imagery that sets Jesus off from the other criminals in the story. He chose not to speak of the resurrection, clearly an important reality in the story,—and he completely missed the irony so crucial to the narrative. But if the particulars—in this case, details that make claims about people and places and times—are crucial to the meaning of the narrative, they cannot be collapsed into the typical or the mythic. They invite not only literary but also historical study.

To ignore questions about referentiality would be to transmute the biblical material into something other than what it is.

4. Perhaps the most promising of the current approaches, John Donahue argues, falls under the heading "rhetorical criticism."[4] Such a discipline has been in the process of gestation for more than two decades. Rhetorical critics share the conviction that biblical literature was written to persuade. That is perhaps most obvious in the case of Paul's letters, but it is only slightly less so with the Gospels. Luke in fact says that he wishes to convince Theophilus of "the certainty of the things you have been taught" (Luke 1:4, NIV). The task of rhetorical analysis is to make clear the argument of a letter or a narrative.

The insights of rhetorical analysis should be broadened to include the whole interpretive enterprise. As critics, we are ourselves engaged in persuasion—specifically, in creating an audience with particular competencies and expectations. At this juncture the whole interpretive enterprise seems to be at an important crossroads. No interpretation is disinterested, as Rudolf Bultmann made clear some time ago. Particularly in the U.S., however, scholarship has proceeded as if it were possible to carry out interpretation without a perspective on basic theological questions—the clearest examples being Stendahl's now-famous article on interpretation[5] or Mary Ann Tolbert's more recent statement of it in her study of the parables in Mark. The result of such descriptive scholarship has been the creation of an audience increasingly distanced from Scripture. Far from being theologically neutral, such biblical scholarship has become antitheological.

In 1975, Nils Dahl wrote "The Neglected Factor in New Testament Theology."[6] The neglected factor, he insists, is God. Scholars have studied Markan soteriology and Christology, but few think about theology—

---

4. John Donahue, "The Changing Shape of New Testament Theology," *Theological Studies* 50 (1989): 314–35.

5. *International Dictionary of the Bible* (Nashville: Abingdon Press, 1962), s.v. "interpretation."

6. See Nils Dahl, *Jesus the Christ* (Minneapolis: Fortress Press, 1991), 153–64.

about God. John Donahue followed his lead with an article on Markan theology, entitled, "A Neglected Factor in the Theology of Mark."[7] Interpreters, these two scholars demonstrate, have created an audience for the Gospels that is uninterested in the question of God. Yet Dahl's and Donahue's arguments could be carried considerably further. It is not simply that the topic of God is never raised; the reality of God is excluded from the imagination of interpreters. To whatever extent modern interpretation effectively exorcises God from public imagination, such scholarship is antitheological, in spite of the intentions of particular interpreters.

In an article entitled "Theological Consensus or Historicist Evasion? Jews and Christians in Biblical Studies," Jon Levenson raises precisely this question in speaking about the contemporary convention of studying Hebrew Bible as opposed to Tanak or Old Testament:

> This meeting of Jews and Christians on neutral grounds can have great value, for it helps to correct misconceptions each group has of the other and to prevent the grievous consequences of such misconceptions, such as anti-Semitic persecutions. It is also the case that some of the insights into the text that historical criticism generates will be appreciated by the Jews or the Church themselves, who can thereby convert history into tradition and add vitality to an exegetical practice become stale and repetitive. But it is also the case that the historical-critical method compels its practitioners to bracket their traditional identities, and this renders its ability to enrich Judaism and Christianity problematic. . . . unless historical criticism can learn to interact with other senses of Scripture—senses peculiar to the individual traditions and not shared between them—it will either fade or prove to be not a meeting ground of Jews and Christians, but the burial ground of Judaism and Christianity, as each tradition vanishes into the past in which neither had as yet emerged.[8]

The so-called bracketing of religious investments has paid dividends of a sort within the academic world. No one would wish to return to a time when the Bible was captive to ecclesiastical authority or when differences of opinion led to bonfires. Yet if we are to entertain the possibility that the Scriptures do wish to make claims on us, and if central to such claims is the conviction that God is at work when we are engaged by the Bible, then the matter of rhetorical strategy among current interpreters must be subjected to scrutiny. I argue throughout

---

7. Donahue, *Journal of Biblical Literature* 101 (1982): 563–94.

8. John Levenson, *Hebrew Bible or Old Testament? Studying the Bible in Judaism and Christianity,* ed. Roger Brooks and John J. Collins (Notre Dame: Univ. of Notre Dame Press, 1990), 110–45, 144.

that one of the principal agendas of current interpretive strategies is to keep the reality of God at bay. One of the great surprises of engagement with Mark may be the discovery that God will not be excluded, that the tearing of the heavens and of the temple curtain may result in an irreparable breach in our own defenses against the real presence the narrative mediates.

The rhetorical strategy I have in mind does not foreclose the possibility of such engagement with Mark's Gospel. That should not imply any privileged status for my interpretations. It does suggest, however, a certain discomfort within the guild to which professional Bible readers belong. When I presented an earlier version of a chapter, one of my colleagues responded, "It's one of the best sermons I've heard on the passage." His remark was more than a little ironic. His appreciation was tempered by a conviction that the rhetorical strategy seemed more appropriate to the pulpit than to the classroom or professional seminar. I have no doubt that so-called disinterested reading is safer. I believe, however, that the price for our comfort is too great. If what moves us to read the Bible is the possibility not just of meaningfulness but of truthfulness, then we have little choice but to weigh anchor and sail out of the harbor into the deep.

2

A Context for Interpretation:
From Papias to Perrin

George Steiner's biting remarks about the harm done to appreciation of the arts by critics who become preoccupied with criticism give more than a little pause in beginning a book with a study of earlier studies.[1] Reading is determined by expectations, however, and we are a product of our prior, persistent expectations. Tradition teaches us what to expect of books, what to seek out, how to prepare for an engagement with a narrative. This can be especially problematic in the case of literature that does not arise from our own culture or that does not abide by the rules we know without thinking about them. Sometimes we need encouragement to try out something that does not look promising—as even college students need to be encouraged to work at a difficult novel, such as Faulkner's *The Sound and the Fury*. In the opening of his *The Genesis of Secrecy*, Frank Kermode suggests that without some reason to take Mark's Gospel seriously as a narrative, few readers would bother— and he is right.[2]

The remarkable fact is that prior to the last few decades, few readers in the history of the church have bothered. Mark's Gospel was the least read of all Gospels. Judged by usage, it is remarkable that the work was transmitted as part of the canon at all. Yet in the last two centuries, the Gospel has received unprecedented attention, and, in the last two decades, the once least read is now perhaps the most studied and appreciated

---

1. See George Steiner, *Real Presences* (Chicago: The Univ. of Chicago Press, 1990), chap. 1.
2. Frank Kermode, *The Genesis of Secrecy: On the Interpretation of Narrative* (Cambridge: Harvard Univ. Press, 1979).

Gospel of the four. Determining the validity of the wide range of claims made for the Gospel and gaining a sense of our bearings as we begin our interpretive expeditions will be enhanced by a sense of what has come before and where scholarship is at the present.

From Papias to the Reformation

Whereas little has received universal agreement, a consensus has emerged that Mark was the first Gospel to be written. At least two attempts were made to displace Mark within a generation of its composition, and these have found their way into the Christian canon. If history provides any evidence, their attempts were largely successful. The Gospel according to Matthew became the church's Gospel in terms of what was read and quoted, and the "Gospel according to Luke" provided at least a neat transition to the history of the early church.

The first explicit, extant comment about Mark was made by Papias of Hierapolis, whose comments on a variety of subjects were recorded by the great historian Eusebius. While every student in introductory Bible classes learns about Papias, most are misled by interpreters of the famous testimonium. A significant difference of opinion exists about how to translate the Greek. The disagreement is important because it determines a starting point for assessing appraisals of Mark in the history of the church. What follows is my own translation, whose small differences from the nearly canonical version in the Loeb Classical Library series merit some attention.

> Mark was the interpreter of Peter. He wrote down accurately, but without form [*ou mentoi taxei*], what he remembered of the things said and done by the Lord. For neither did he hear the Lord, nor did he follow him, but later on, as I said, Peter—who fashioned the teachings according to the needs of the moment, but not as though he were drawing up a connected account of the Lord's sayings. Thus Mark made no mistake in thus recording some things as he remembered them. For he had one thing in mind, namely to omit nothing of the things he had heard and to falsify nothing among them.

Most significant is the sense of the Greek *taxis* ("order"). What does Papias mean by "Mark wrote down accurately but not *taxei* . . ."? Most have read the comment as historical in character, indicating an opinion about Mark's chronological structuring of Jesus' ministry. Josef Kürzinger was to my knowledge the first to suggest that the phrase ought to be understood within a rhetorical setting as implying a lack of form.[3]

---

3. Joseph Kürzinger, "Die Aussage des Papias von Hierapolis zur literarischen Form des Markusevangeliums," BZ 21 (1977), 245–64.

Mark has no *taxis*—the kind of order one expects from a piece of literature. Papias' comments should be read, Kürzinger argues, as an explanation of and an apology for Mark's perceived aesthetic failings. The work ought not be judged by such standards, he suggests, because Mark had no literary pretensions. Mark's Gospel should be read as the publication of an interpreter's notes. The sources of his information were occasional presentations by Peter, who likewise never set out to narrate a story. Although the matter of authorization may lie behind Papias' brief comments—who was Mark to write a Gospel?— the major concern is aesthetic: the book known as The Gospel according to Mark does not measure up to contemporary standards. It is not literature. It has no form, no "style."[4]

Papias' comments have had an enormous impact on the history of Markan interpretation within the church. It does not matter whether or not opinions of various church fathers can be traced directly to Papias. What is important is that the suggestions—that Mark is somehow tied to St. Peter, that the book has no literary form, and that it elicits confidence in its faithfulness and accuracy—have shaped the expectations of successive generations of Bible readers. The prominent place accorded Papias' testimony in the *Synopsis Quatuor Evangeliorum* and in introductory texts—framed within a particular translation and interpretation—has ensured a kind of immortality for a view that, as many have already concluded, is unwarranted.

Mark's place in the early Christian church is thus hardly surprising. A brief survey of citation indices among various church fathers is itself sufficient evidence that the Gospel according to Mark was little read. The topic deserves more careful scrutiny, but one may suspect that detailed investigation will confirm initial hunches.

The matter of usage is, of course, complex. Not unimportant is that the Scriptures were employed piecemeal. The development of lectionaries largely determined how the Bible would be employed in public (which was the only way most believers encountered it). The reading in bits and pieces meant that content was primary. We have little evidence

---

4. Other features of Kürzinger's argument merit discussion. His case would be strengthened, for example, if the phrase *pros tas chreias* could be translated "in the manner of 'Chreia,' " that is, in the fashion of collections of pithy sayings, like the famous "Chreiai of Socrates" by Zeno. Using the Ibicus computer, my colleagues and I surveyed the entire corpus of Greek literature currently on the *Thesaurus Linguae Graecae* (the RAM disk prepared at the University of California Irvine). We found thirty-six occurrences of the expression *pros tas chreias*, of which only three were related to Papias' comment. In every instance, the phrase must be translated in the conventional manner, "as needs dictate." This observation does not substantially weaken Kürzinger's argument, however.

that whole narratives were performed or that they functioned as narratives. Even though literary evidence from the history of the church needs to be supplemented with evidence of liturgical practice and popular piety, little doubt can remain that our ancestors read biblical works rather differently, with a different theory of how texts work. The midrashic mind-set—interest in the sentences and letters of the sacred text, known principally from Jewish commentaries—was as dominant among Christian interpreters as among other readers of sacred texts in the ancient world.[5] The road to the fourfold method of interpretation in the Middle Ages was already paved. Even speaking about the Gospels as narratives may thus be misleading in terms of their actual operation in the church.

Evidence does exist of interest in whole Gospels. In this regard, Augustine's brief treatment of Mark is instructive. He discusses the Gospel and its relationship to the other accounts of Jesus' ministry in his *Treatise on the Harmony of the Gospels*. From the outset, his interest in Mark is bound up with the problem of the multiplicity of the Gospels. At a commonsense level, disagreements pose problems (in Jewish tradition, the matter was discussed under the formal heading, "Contradictions in the Scriptures"). The issue had less to do with a passion for historical accuracy than with authorization of a work as trustworthy. The problem of authorship is of obvious concern. Whereas each of the Gospels was written under the inspiration of the Spirit, according to Augustine, the apostolic authorship of at least two needs to be acknowledged. Whereas Jesus chose twelve disciples to preach, Augustine points out that only two were to write books:

> But as respects the task of composing that record of the gospel which is to be accepted as ordained by divine authority, there were (only) two, belonging to the number of those whom the Lord chose before the passover, that obtained places—namely, the first place and the last. And thus the remaining two, who did not belong to the referred to, but who at the same time had become followers of the Christ who spoke in these others, were supported on either side by the same, the sons who were to be embraced, and who in this way were set in the midst between the twain.[6]

Of Mark in particular, Augustine comments:

> Mark follows him [Matthew] closely like his attendant and epitomizer. For in his narrative he gives nothing in concert with John apart from

5. See the work of Karlfried Froehlich, *Biblical Interpretation in the Early Church* (Philadelphia: Fortress Press, 1984).

6. Augustine, *Treatise on the Harmony of the Gospels* II, 3 in *Nicene and Post-Nicene Fathers*, ed. Philip Schaff (New York: Scribners, 1903), 6:78.

the others; by himself separately, he has little to record; in conjunction with Luke, as distinguished from the rest, he has still less; but in concord with Matthew, he has a very large number of passages. Much, too, he narrates in words almost numerically and identically the same as those used by Matthew, where the agreement is either with that evangelist alone, or with him in connection with the rest.[7]

Augustine's basic outline for his *Harmony* is taken from Matthew. Distinctive material is viewed as requiring explanation. In book IV, where he discusses material peculiar to Mark, Luke, and John, the only passages considered are those that give the appearance of contradicting Matthew. The reference to the naked young man in Mark 14, for example, is noted without comment, for while it is unique to Mark, it contradicts nothing in Matthew or Luke.

The success of Augustine's justification of Mark's presence in the canon and his characterization of Mark as Matthew's epitomizer—or perhaps the clarity with which he articulated common opinion—can be observed in the extraordinary absence of citations of Mark in subsequent Christian writings prior to the Enlightenment.

Even without particular theories about the relationship of the Gospels, reading practices encouraged harmonizing the Gospels. Thus Mark became unimportant largely because it included so little distinctive material. Virtually everything in Mark could be found in Matthew or Luke. The distinctive material in Mark—such as the comment of Jesus' relatives that he was out of his mind (Mark 3:21) or the sayings about being salted with fire (9:49-50)—were of little interest. The only peculiarly Markan features to attract attention are the note about the young boy running naked from Jesus' arrest (Mark 14:51-52) and material from the spurious ending.

As far as is visible to us, Augustine offers insight into the way the Gospels actually functioned (and were to function) within the church, and his suggestions about the relationship of Mark to Matthew deal with implied criticism that need no longer be of concern to the faithful (that is, Why are there four Gospels? Who was Mark?). Mark now assumes a new role among Christian academics: He is Matthew's epitomizer whose summary might be of interest to others but not to the serious scholar who has time to read Matthew's lengthier version.

The triumph of Augustine's approach to Mark is again apparent in the mere statistics available in indices of scriptural quotations. For example, St. Francis, so far as we can tell, does not allude to Mark a single time in his recorded writings.

7. *Harmony* II, 4; Schaff, p. 78.

Calvin wrote commentaries on every book in the New Testament. His commentary on Mark, however, is part of a commentary on the harmony of Matthew, Mark, and Luke.[8] Interestingly, Calvin did not agree that Mark was simply an abridgment of Matthew:

> There is no ground whatever for the statement of Jerome, that his Gospel is an abridgement of the Gospel of Matthew. He does not everywhere adhere to the order which Matthew observed, and from the very commencement handles the subject in a different manner. Some things, too, are related by him which the other had omitted, and his narrative of the same event is sometimes more detailed. It is more probable . . . that he had not seen Matthew's book when he wrote his own.[9]

Crucial to Calvin was that the subject matter in Mark owes its authority to the inspiration of the Spirit. The few pieces of distinctive material are little more than curiosities, and the peculiar form of Mark is of little consequence because Matthew and Luke provide the information needed to fashion the story Calvin interprets in his harmony.

In dealing with the ending of Mark, Calvin arranges his commentary with a break after 16:7. Verse 8 is read with verses 9-12. Calvin's reading must be close to the way the passage was heard by most interpreters:

> Yet there is some diversity in the words of Mark . . . so that through fear they were dismayed. But the solution is not very difficult; for though they were resolved to obey the angel, still they had not the power to do so, if the Lord himself had not loosed their tongues.[10]

The ending of the Gospel is a matter of particular significance.[11] The decision about what verses are printed as the ending of Mark has a bearing on how the Gospel was read and what impact it made—as well as on how the Gospel is read today and what impact it makes. Some helpful surveys are available on the history of the Markan ending.[12] Most striking is that whereas such scholars as Jerome knew of versions of Mark that lacked verses 9-20, his Vulgate, which became the official Bible for the whole of Western Christendom, printed a version that included the verses. Prior to the publication of Tischendorf's Greek New Testament, no readers had access to a printed version of Mark's

---

8. *Calvin's Commentaries: Harmony of Matthew, Mark, and Luke*, trans. Rev. W. Pringle (Grand Rapids: Baker, 1979), vols. 16, 17.

9. *Calvin's Commentaries* 16:38.

10. *Calvin's Commentaries* 17:347.

11. The interrelationship of textual criticism and interpretation will be considered in another chapter 8.

12. The most complete discussion and bibliography is available in the commentary by R. Pesch, *Das Markusevangelium*, 2 vols., HNTKNT 2 (Freiburg: Herder, 1976–77).

Gospel that ended with verse 8. That is surely a significant matter for understanding the Gospel's place in the history of interpretation.

That the greatest impact Mark's Gospel has made on church tradition is derived from verses which no modern textual critic would acknowledge as belonging to Mark is no small matter. Among Luther's allusions to Mark in his collected works, almost one fourth are to passages from the spurious ending (16:9-20). The single verse from Mark that has achieved fame because of its place in Luther's Small Catechism—"Whoever believes and is baptized shall be saved" (16:16)—is from the spurious ending.[13]

The history of interpretation of Mark, perhaps more than with most New Testament works, is tied to the discipline of textual criticism and to decisions of Bible publishers about which book will be read under the heading, "The Gospel according to St. Mark." To this day, no Bible makes available to readers a version of Mark's Gospel in which the spurious endings are so designated in an unambiguous way.[14] The scribes who formulated the endings, particularly the so-called longer ending, still determine for most people how the Gospel according to Mark will be read.

The Modern Era

The rebirth of interest in Mark (if it is appropriate to imply that a former era was interested) begins with the dawning of historical consciousness—or, to put it another way, with the increasingly respectable suspicion among the learned that things were not always as they had been told. The need to provide foundations for beliefs that had survived for generations with the support of institutionalized authority simply exacerbated that suspicion. Surveys of the rise of the historical Jesus movement nicely document the shift in conceptuality.

In such a setting, Mark suddenly became interesting—and for many of the same reasons it had been ignored. A significant moment in the history of research was the determination that Mark was the first of the

---

13. The verse is cited in the second section in Luther's explanation of baptism. See Theodore Tappert, trans. and ed., "The Small Catechism, *The Book of Concord* (Philadelphia: Fortress Press, 1959), 349.

14. I find particularly unconscionable the decision of the NRSV to print the "alternative" endings as though they had the same status as the rest of the text. The use of double brackets and footnotes (which few will read) does nothing to correct the impression of most Bible readers that one must choose between the "longer ending" and the "shorter ending" of the Gospel.

Gospels to have been written. Yet even prior to that conviction, which was not suggested until 1838[15] and was not made respectable until H. J. Holtzmann became a principal advocate, readers became intrigued by a feature of Mark's narrative that we may call its history-likeness. Even before the establishment of Markan priority had been convincingly argued, J. G. Herder had observed of Mark that

> no other Gospel has so little of the authorial and so much of the lively tone of the narrator as this one. Mark is closer to the style of oral tradition than the other two [synoptics] in the material they share. His easy manner of spinning a yarn, coupled with loose connections, corresponds to the manner in which material is customarily formed in the speech of ordinary people. His language is popular, original and artless, robust and rough, with a decidedly Aramaic flavor.[16]

Stories carried conviction. Mark alone relishes small details. The Gerasene demoniac had been bound with both chains and fetters (not just chains, as in Matthew). He broke the chains and ripped apart the fetters (5:4). The woman with the hemorrhage had spent all her money on physicians and had not gotten better but worse (5:25-34). When Jesus took the little girl by the hand, he said, *"Talitha cum"* (5:22-24, 35-43); when he put his fingers into the ears of the deaf mute, he said *"Ephphatha"* (7:34)—Aramaic phrases Mark's readers would not have understood. Mark translates the phrases, but their very presence offers a sense of authenticity. Taken together with the apparent lack of artistic sophistication, these features suggested to many the sure marks of oral tradition—and, in that regard, of proximity to the events themselves.

Differences of opinion regarding the veracity of Mark's accounts did arise. Christian Weisse, who first began using Mark as the primary source

---

15. The first evidence that Matthew reworked Mark and not vice versa was suggested by Christian Gottlieb Wilke in "Über die Parabel von den Arbeitern im Weinberg Matth. 20.1–16," *Wiener Zeitschrift für wissenschaftliche Theologie* I (1826): 73–88, further developed in his *Der Urevangelist* (1838). The argument for the priority of the Markan order was suggested by Carl Lachmann, "De ordine narrationum in evangeliis synopticis," TSK 8 (1835): 570–90. Whereas Lachmann argued only that Mark was the mediating feature between Matthew and Luke (thus leaving open the question of an even earlier source of Mark), Wilke provided detailed exegetical support for the theory that Mark was the first (Wellhausen, *Einleitung in die drei ersten Evangelien,* 2d ed. [1911], 35–36). The exploitation of this observation for reconstructing the history of Jesus was initiated by Christian Hermann Weisse in his *Die evangelische Geschichte kritisch und philosophisch bearbeitet* (1838). The respectability of Markan priority was established by Holtzmann in his *Die synoptischen Evangelien* (Leipzig: Wilhelm Engelmann, 1863).

16. Quoted and translated from Wellhausen, *Einleitung,* 37.

for reconstructing the history of Jesus, was by no means uncritical in his assessment of the history-like narrative. Albert Schweitzer comments:

> He is far from having used Mark unreservedly as a historical source. On the contrary, he says expressly that the picture which this Gospel gives of Jesus is drawn by an imaginative disciple of the faith, filled with the glory of his subject, whose enthusiasm is consequently sometimes stronger than his judgment. Even in Mark the mythopoeic tendency is already actively at work, so that often the task of historical criticism is to explain how such myths could have been accepted by a reporter who stands as near the facts as Mark does.[17]

The particular problem is not so much the individual episodes as their arrangement.

> The inventor of the Marcan hypothesis never wearies of repeating that even in the Second Gospel it is only the main outline of the Life of Jesus, not the way in which the various sections are joined together, which is historical. He does not, therefore, venture to write a Life of Jesus, but begins with a "General Sketch of the Gospel History" in which he gives the main outlines of the life of Jesus according to Mark, and then proceeds to explain the incidents and discourses in each several Gospel in the order in which they occur.[18]

Respect for the narrative's verisimilitude is tempered by a sense that the narrative lacks order and structure, reminiscent of Papias' views centuries earlier.

For those Bible readers most interested in historical questions, the combination of convincing stories and apparent lack of style in overall construction have served as evidence of Mark's reliability as a source. The view is nicely articulated by Vincent Taylor in his famous commentary on Mark. Writing as late as the 1950s, he represents the scholarly perspective that developed over a century and a half. Striking, according to Taylor, are the "vivid details" in Mark.

> If the vivid details in Mark are original, they are of the greatest importance in assessing its historical value. In themselves lifelike touches are not a sure criterion, since they may be due to the exercise of a vivid imagination, but they present data on which a judgment may be based, especially if their character and distribution are considered.[19]

17. Quoted in A. Schweitzer, *The Quest of the Historical Jesus,* trans. W. Montgomery from *Von Reimarus zu Wrede* (New York: Macmillan, 1961).

18. Schweitzer, *Quest,* 131.

19. Vincent Taylor, *The Gospel according to St. Mark* (London: Macmillan, 1963; 1st ed., 1952), 135.

Taylor proceeds to list dozens of these "vivid details" from the opening six chapters, while noting that details are absent from other passages (especially "Markan constructions"). The results seem apparent:

> The explanation can only be that for these narratives Mark was dependent on fragmentary tradition and did not attempt to colour it, that he is not a creative writer comparable to Luke or John. But if so, the limitations of Mark point to his fidelity to tradition. In his stories about Jesus and his miracle-stories the wealth of detail is given, not created. His objectivity is a sign of the highest historical value of the Gospel.[20]

Echoes of Papias' testimony figure prominently in Taylor's argument:

> Separated at the time of writing by little more than a generation from the death of Jesus, its contents carry us back farther into the oral period before Mark wrote to the tradition first of the Palestinian community and subsequently that of the Gentile Church at Rome. The historical value of Mark depends upon the Evangelist's fidelity to that tradition, including his special advantages as a hearer of Peter's preaching.[21]

Taylor stands squarely within a remarkable tradition of interpretation that had developed among enlightened Bible readers. On the one hand, learned exegetes acknowledged what Papias had noted: Mark lacked literary sophistication, as evidenced not only by the barbarous Greek but also by the gaps in the story and the episodic prose. On the other hand, these exegetes were taken by the history-likeness of that prose. The only reasonable conclusion seemed to be that Mark "wrote down accurately, but without form, what Jesus said and did." Mark's aesthetic shortcomings demonstrate the historical veracity of his work.[22]

Such conclusions were at odds with some of the trends in nineteenth-century scholarship. Bruno Bauer and Wilhelm Wrede, for example, had much invested in the creativity of the tradition, particularly that of Mark. Yet, according to Schweitzer's assessment of their work, even they were unable to sustain a reading of Mark that rendered it coherent. Schweitzer believed that Mark had the story right, although he recorded

---

20. *Ibid.*, 140.
21. *Ibid.*, 148.
22. Wellhausen expresses the idea forcefully:
Mark undoubtedly intended to record the whole tradition, with the stories about Jesus as well as his words. It is impossible to assume that he did not take up completely everything from the tradition that was accessible to him or that he omitted what had already been recorded. He is nothing less than a supplementer. If without or contrary to his intent this or that escaped him, these gleanings of old and genuine material that he left for others do not produce a yield disproportionally richer than his own harvest. (*Einleitung*, 77)

the facts without the faintest idea what held them together or made sense of them because only Jesus' uniquely eschatological perspective held the story together—and rendered it unserviceable for all future generations. Schweitzer speaks for most of twentieth-century scholarship when he offers his assessment of Markan interpretation up to his own day:

> Here we recognize also why the Marcan hypothesis, in constructing its view of the Life of Jesus, found itself obliged to have recourse more and more to the help of modern psychology, and thus necessarily became more and more unhistorical. The fact which alone makes possible an understanding of the whole, is lacking in this Gospel. Without [Matt.] 10 and 11 everything remains enigmatic. For this reason Bruno Bauer and Wrede are in their own way the only consistent representatives of the Marcan hypothesis from the point of view of historical criticism, when they arrive at the result that the Marcan account is inherently unintelligible.[23]

Yet Schweitzer and most of his predecessors could believe at the same time that Mark was historically reliable. His stories had the feel of authenticity.

While much of twentieth-century scholarship has become far more suspicious than Schweitzer of Mark's historical reliability, scholars have shared his view of the Gospel's literary failings. The well-known evaluation of Martin Dibelius and Karl Ludwig Schmidt—that the Gospels are only collections of material, and that without the flimsy framework the author imposes on his material the narrative disintegrates—dominated not only published scholarship but also the educational enterprise within which the next generation of scholars was trained. The dominance of source-critical questions rendered many trained Bible readers incapable of following a story.

For much of biblical scholarship in this century, not the story, but something else mattered. In academic circles, the dominance of an essentially Romantic view of interpretation was almost overwhelming. Those scholars who had been forced to abandon the attempt to get at the mind of Jesus turned instead to the religious community. It was the genius, the spirit, of the primitive Christian groups who had for a decade or two preserved the sayings and deeds of Jesus in oral form, with which interpreters hoped to establish contact. The shift to redaction criticism in the 1950s did not mark an essential change hermeneutically. Those young scholars like Hans Conzelmann and Marxsen who had been

---

23. Schweitzer, *Quest*, 360.

trained in source criticism simply substituted the mind of Mark or the mind of Luke for that of the primitive communities. The goal of interpretation was to penetrate behind the narrative or letter to something that promised inspiration and stability—the personality of the genius who had edited the Jesus tradition so as to fix it for all generations.[24]

The shortcomings of the Romantic hermeneutic have been amply exposed in the last two decades of hermeneutical reflection.[25] The source-critical approach to reading narratives has likewise been subjected to considerable scrutiny and critique. Yet, focus on the person of the authors has done little to provide stability for interpreters. Particularly with respect to Mark, the real author and his views remain hidden behind a hundred guesses. Further, the premise of redaction criticism, that one can know an author best by noting where he disagrees with the tradition he edits, is highly one sided and will even in the most favorable of circumstances yield no satisfying or convincing portrait.[26] Finally, form and redaction criticism have done little to enhance the reading of the Scriptures themselves. Several prominent redaction critics studied the trial of Jesus before the Sanhedrin in Mark 14 without even noting correspondences between this account and the narrative of Jesus' death. This is itself adequate demonstration of how thoroughly the source-critical preoccupation had incapacitated interpreters.[27] The issue is not whether a genetic explanation of the Gospel narratives is valid; the issue is to what extent it passes for interpretation.[28]

The Perrin School

Perhaps no other scholar as clearly marks the transition from the historical and the source-critical to the literary-critical phase of Markan

24. The goal of redactional studies was not always positive. One might suggest that Conzelmann studied Luke's Gospel to establish contact with Luke, so as to dismiss quite thoroughly the evangelist's non-eschatological, historicizing perspective.

25. For a discussion, see Patrick Keifert, "Meaning and Reference: The Interpretation of Verisimilitude in the Gospel according to Mark" (Ph.D diss., University of Chicago, 1982), esp. 46–59, 143–46.

26. For a clear summary of the critique of Redaction Criticism, see David Moessner, *Lord of the Banquet* (Minneapolis: Fortress Press, 1989), 4–7.

27. Among prominent interpreters one might include Eduard Schweizer, Eta Linnemann, and Johannes Schreiber—all of whom produced studies of Jesus' trial before the Jewish court from the perspective of redaction criticism. For a critique, see Juel, *Messiah and Temple*, 25–29.

28. The matter has been analyzed in an incisive manner by such scholars as Meier Sternberg, *The Poetics of Biblical Narrative: Ideological Literature and the Drama of Reading*, Indiana Literary Biblical Series (Bloomington, Ind.: Indiana Univ. Press, 1985).

scholarship as does Norman Perrin. His career began with his doctoral work under T. W. Manson on the Jesus tradition. Always a restless and a daring scholar, Perrin soon became convinced that Bultmann had been correct in his debate with Jeremias about the teachings of Jesus. Perrin became more skeptical about what could be known about Jesus, and he later wrote studies on the Son of Man in which he argued that we cannot know if Jesus ever used the expression and that in any case the strange Greek phrase came to be part of the Christian tradition through the interpretation of Scripture, notably Daniel 7:14.[29] With the advent of redaction criticism, Perrin began his own studies on Mark, which came to include a number of talented young graduate students. His dominating influence on the Mark seminar in the Society of Biblical Literature resulted in significant changes in the direction of Markan scholarship across the country.

Perrin's solid historical training and his expertise in Jewish interpretive tradition were supplemented by a growing appreciation for the more subtle literary and hermeneutical arts practiced at the University of Chicago. His little study *What Is Redaction Criticism?* marks a significant departure from earlier European methodological purity. While continuing to employ *source criticism* (the distinguishing of tradition and redaction, to use the technical terminology), he became increasingly interested in literary analysis in the more widely understood sense outside the narrow field of biblical scholarship.

> The fundamental premise of redaction criticism, then, is that the pericope can be analyzed from the perspective of a Marcan purpose. The goal of such an analysis is to understand the purpose and the theology that is revealed in the purpose. To this end we concern ourselves both with the individual parts of the narrative and with the story as a whole. In other words, we analyze the constituent parts of the narrative . . . to see what they tell us of Mark as one who gathers, modifies, or creates tradition, and we analyze the total narrative in terms of its overall purposes . . . to see what this will tell us about Mark as an evangelist.[30]

What he came to describe as redaction criticism was something quite different from Marxsen's enterprise, with regard both to the

---

29. Norman Perrin, "Mark 14:62: The End Product of a Christian Pesher Tradition?" NTS 12 (1966): 150–55; and "The Creative Use of the Son of Man Traditions in Mark," USQR 23 (1967–68): 357–65.

30. Norman Perrin, *What Is Redaction Criticism?* (Philadelphia: Fortress Press, 1969), 42.

method and goal of interpretation.[31] In regard to method, Perrin could write later:

> But now I have reached the methodological point of recognizing that so far as the interpretation of Mk is concerned questions of tradition and redaction are comparatively unimportant: what matters is the *function* of the text concerned in the Gospel as a whole.[32]

In regard to the goal of redaction criticism, Perrin's interest in Mark was to correlate more thoroughly theological perspective and historical situation:

> If redaction criticism helps us to determine more and more exactly the theological developments in earliest Christianity, then it will be natural for us to ask ourselves what historical circumstances lie behind these theological developments. It may well be then that redaction criticism itself will ultimately produce a theological history of earliest Christianity such as it has not yet been possible to write.[33]

Perrin never did abandon his interest and investment in historical study, but his exegetical work on Mark came to focus more and more on literary matters. That has surely been true in the work of his students who have come increasingly to identify the narrative itself as the locus of interpretation. The world in front of the text became the focal point of interpretation. To speak of Mark is not necessarily to refer either to the flesh and blood figure about whom we know virtually nothing or the fragmentary perspective that results from a separation of tradition and redaction, identifying Mark with the redactional perspective alone. What is meant by *Mark* in Perrin's latest work is the *implied author* of the Gospel—the sum total of the judgments and points of view that emerge from a reading of the work.

Historical questions were not abandoned by Perrin's students. Werner Kelber's thesis depended upon a construct of early Christian history in which the future was important both as a religious and a political matter.[34] The work of Vernon Robbins and Mary Ann Tolbert locates the Gospel within the literary and rhetorical conventions of the Greco-Roman world.[35] But new questions had been asked that needed to be

31. For an analysis and critique of Marxsen's essentially romantic hermeneutic, see Keifert, "Meaning and Reference," 108–23.

32. Perrin, "The High Priest's Question and Jesus' Answer," *The Passion in Mark*, ed. Werner Kelber (Philadelphia: Fortress Press, 1976), 90.

33. *Ibid.*, 39; see also 78–79 and his comment on "redaction criticism" in *The New Testament: An Introduction* (New York: Harcourt, Brace, Jovanovich, 1974), 13.

34. Werner Kelber, *The Kingdom in Mark* (Philadelphia: Fortress Press, 1974).

35. Vernon Robbins, *Jesus the Teacher: A Socio-Rhetorical Interpretation of Mark* (Philadelphia: Fortress Press, 1984); Mary Ann Tolbert, *Sowing the Gospel*.

sorted out. Mark was read as something quite different from the artless collection of material earlier generations had seen.

The Present Scene

Major shifts have failed to win a consensus. Views have rather proliferated. Publications continue to feature work that is as historicist as anything in the nineteenth century. Practitioners of pure redaction criticism still are convinced that interpretation must begin with the separation of tradition and redaction. Yet important shifts have provided a new context for interpretation.

1. Virtual agreement exists among students of the Bible that Mark's Gospel is worth reading as a narrative. The failure to agree on some ancient genre on the basis of which to understand the Markan narrative does not lead most contemporary readers of Mark to Papias' conclusion that the Gospel is utterly lacking in artfulness. There is a consensus that interpreters ought to focus on the whole cloth and not on separate threads—and that such efforts will be rewarded. Although disagreements may arise about what it means to appreciate a narrative and about the sorts of claims narratives can make, few today read the earliest Gospel without feeling obliged to attend to Mark's story as a whole.

2. The Romantic hermeneutic no longer represents the dominant interpretive strategy. Whereas scholars may still speak of the "intention of the author," they generally have in mind something different from the thoughts and feelings of a flesh and blood evangelist named Mark. Booth, Wolfgang Iser, and others have convincingly argued that if we are to speak about author's intention at all, we need to understand that we are speaking first about the *implied author*—the sum total of the judgments and outlook that result from literary analysis rather than historical reconstruction. While some still read the Gospel confident that stories furnish direct contact with "Mark" or the Christian community or even "Jesus," few make such assumptions naively, and their arguments carry less conviction.

3. The problem of history has been posed in a new way. There are numerous interpreters who would like to dispense with the whole problem of history altogether by focusing questions of truth and meaning on narrative matters alone. Even the most committed formalists, however, rely on historical reconstructions of the first century to determine the possible range of meaning for various Greek terms and expressions. Scriptural allusions require some sense of how the Old Testament was read and interpreted.

Further, however difficult the problem of referentiality may be, attending to the Gospel requires assessments of various sorts. Scholars have used the image of parable to characterize not simply those figures in Mark so identified, but the narrative itself.[36] Yet there are common-sense differences between, say, the "parables" in chapter 4 and the passion narrative. Readers do not feel impelled to ask for the name of the sower or the location of the field. The parable makes no such referential claims; the truth of the parable does not require such an identification. In the passion narrative, however, the Gospel makes numerous referential claims; times, names, and places become important. The striking identification of Simon as "the father of Alexander and Rufus" claims to be true in the usual sense of referring to someone who actually existed. Failing to distinguish between the truth claims of parables and of history-like narrative is an unacceptable solution to the problem of history in Mark. In this regard, the questions posed by James Robinson have not been sufficiently addressed.[37]

Historical questions have not been solved or dismissed, but they have been shifted to a different point in the argument. For most contemporary interpreters, historical realities to which the narrative refers are not the solid pilings on which interpretations can be built. The goal of reading is the world in front of the text and not the world behind it. The data that hold the greatest promise for stabilizing interpretations are found

36. John R. Donahue, "Jesus as Parable of God in the Gospel of Mark," *Interpretation* 32 (1978): 369–86; *The Gospel as Parable* (Philadelphia: Fortress Press, 1988), 194–99; Werner Kelber, *The Oral and the Written Gospel* (Philadelphia: Fortress Press, 1983), 211–20. Mary Ann Tolbert discusses this assessment (*Sowing the Gospel*, 55–59). Insofar as "parable" is taken in the modern sense as figuratively designating the "paradoxical, open-ended, and participatory nature of the Christian message" (p. 57), it is legitimate. She is unwilling to employ the term as appropriate within the cultural and historical setting of the first century. Her criticism, therefore, has nothing to do with the problem of historical referentiality.

Interesting in her work is the separation of reader-response approaches to interpretation from more historically located methods. Her own attempt to locate the Markan audience in its rhetorical-cultural milieu belongs to the latter. She is remarkably reticent to suggest in what sense her work provides any necessary constraints on interpretations that intend to make sense of Mark in the present. In this regard, she does not seem to have freed herself from the Stendahlian construct of "meant/means" despite her assurances (p. 57).

37. *The Problem of History in Mark* (Chatham, England: SCM Press, 1957). Robinson's question has to do with his observations that Mark intends to write history. While appreciating the eschatological and the existential dimensions of the message, Robinson nevertheless insists that "Mark's understanding of Christian existence consists in an understanding of history: the history of Jesus and the history of the Church" (85). Assessment of Mark's work must therefore include some attention to the form of that work, namely historical narrative.

within the Gospel narrative itself; engagement with the stories results in changing us. Yet historical study has a critical role to play. History can provide constraints on imaginative readings of the text: Given knowledge of the first century, some readings are implausible.[38] Further, historical reconstruction is an indispensable feature in the assessment of the narrative's truthfulness. Even though studying biblical narratives as one would study other literature has proven fruitful, the category *fiction* is inadequate as an appreciation of the Gospel's truthfulness.[39]

4. It should come as no surprise that interpretation of Mark is caught up in larger social, political, and religious currents. Questions are posed for us by our environment, and these questions change. There are significant shifts in what kinds of arguments will persuade. For many in the nineteenth century, interpretation had to be grounded on historical fact. We have become aware that the alleged foundations are really shifting sands. For redaction critics like Marxsen, the goal of interpretation was to encounter the genius of another human being. That creative personality seemed to offer the promise of the reality and stability on which interpreters could build. The domination of the psychological and the personal has taken a beating in the last decades. If personality is no longer regarded as the reality on which life can be constructed—if the Romantic hermeneutic has lost its power to convince—what does provide stability? What will constitute an interpretation that offers conviction? The answers are numerous.

The dominance of the social sciences in current scholarship might suggest that if it is not the *Geist* of the early communities, then it is the structures of its symbolic universe and their embodiment in a particular society that will be convincing and salutary. That may lead to a conviction that *deep structures*, permanent ways of organizing, are revealed in the Scriptures, structures that should be embodied in the present. Others

---

38. This approach is preferable to that of A. E. Harvey, *Jesus and the Constraints of History* (Philadelphia: Westminster Press, 1982). The helpful title of the book obscures confusion about priorities. Harvey begins with historical reconstruction, then does exegesis. The process should be the reverse.

39. See the helpful discussion of "Fiction and History" in Sternberg, *Poetics*, 23–35; see also Keifert, "Meaning and Reference," chapter 5. A good contrast is Mary Ann Tolbert, *Sowing the Gospel*, p. 25: The Gospel is fiction. While unwilling to dismiss questions of historical referentiality, the force of her comments suggests that continuing preoccupation with historical questions by authors like Hans Frei and George Lindbeck (neo-conservatives, as she categorizes them) is genuinely wrong headed: "Such an abuse of literary criticism must not be allowed to destroy its potential value for biblical scholarship."

may insist that there are no stable structures, only contemporary appropriations—perhaps nothing more than private interpretations of the scriptural narratives.[40]

The point is that something is at stake in the interpretive enterprise, something that cannot be separated out from the fabric of human experience. We seek answers to questions and the filling of needs. And it is not enough to read in private. Interpretations are rhetorical exercises intended to convince someone of something—even if that something is little more than my right to hold my own opinions. While fascination with interpretation can become narcissistic, as George Steiner warns,[41] some attention to the rhetorical enterprise is useful—at least so that we can understand the reason that we are making arguments, whom we hope to convince, and of what.

Good News or Its Appearance?

In our appreciation of Mark's Gospel, we are a long way from Bishop Papias. It may be we are just as far from our forebears of two generations ago. The plethora of studies on the earliest of the Gospels suggests that readers have sensed something compelling in the narrative, which opens with a promise of good news. That Mark's disjointed narrative should at this point in history grasp the imagination of Bible readers is susceptible of more than one reading. We might find Mark's Gospel intriguing because it is the most pliant of the Gospel narratives, most susceptible to interpretations by which we make sense of an increasingly complex and senseless world. The fascination with the occult and the enigmatic may betray a need that has the force of instinct, as one of the characters in Umberto Eco's *Foucault's Pendulum* comes to suspect:

> Nothing can dispel from my mind the most reassuring thought that this world is the creation of a shadowy god whose shadow I prolong. Faith

40. That would seem to be the message of the deconstructionists. Such notions, further, are attractive to those minorities whose experiences have been systematically excluded from the interpretive enterprise. See Elizabeth Schüssler Fiorenza, *In Memory of Her: A Feminist Theological Reconstruction of Christian Origins* (New York: Crossroad, 1985). The consequences, however, are not attractive. A glimpse at an agenda of professional Bible society conventions suggests that the reigning interpretive approaches arise from a declaration of independence for individual Bible readers and a surrender of any hope of building a stable consensus.

There does seem to be a growing restlessness with the domination of the individual reader, however. Where such restlessness leads remains to be seen.

41. Steiner, *Real Presences*, chap. 1.

leads to Absolute Optimism . . . If belief is necessary, let it be in a religion that doesn't make you feel guilty. A religion out of joint, fuming, sub-terranean, without an end. Like a novel, not like a theology.

Five paths to a single destination. What a waste. Better a labyrinth that leads everywhere and nowhere. To die with style, live in the Baroque . . .

But what if there is no cosmic Plan? What a mockery, to live in exile when no one sent you there. Exile from a place, moreover, that does not exist.

And what if there is a Plan, but it has eluded you—and will elude you for all eternity?

When religion fails, art provides. You invent the Plan, metaphor of the Unknowable One. Even a human plot can fill the void . . .

Believe there is a secret and you will feel like an initiate. It costs nothing.

To create an immense hope that can never be uprooted, because it has no root. Ancestors who do not exist will never appear and say that you have betrayed. A religion you can keep while betraying it infinitely.[42]

Frank Kermode has invested considerable effort demonstrating how clearly that kind of interpreting has characterized academic studies of Mark.[43] He insinuates that literature like Mark's Gospel generates se-crecy, not secrets, and that the only way interpreters can satisfy their need for order and structure is to impose them onto the narrative by means of cunning and violence.[44] His published reading of Mark is an argument about the nature of reality. It seeks to expose the false promise of good news in Mark's Gospel that will leave the hopeful disappointed in the end. Whereas the immense hope generated by the secret can never be uprooted, it will produce little that is capable of sustaining lives.

On the other hand, the sense of profound irony and disappointment that characterizes public life in the present could be precisely what the Gospel interprets and addresses.[45] The disjointedness of Mark's narrative

42. Eco, *Foucault's Pendulum* (New York: Ballantine Books, 1988 [English translation, 1989]), 434.

43. Frank Kermode, *Genesis of Secrecy.*

44. For a more extended account of Kermode's reading of Mark and a counter-argument, see "The Matter of the Ending," chap. 6 in this volume.

45. Hans Jonas, *The Gnostic Religion: The Message of the Alien God and the Beginning of Christianity* (2d. Eng. ed; Boston: Beacon Press, 1963), includes an appendix on the relationship between Gnosticism and Existentialism. Jonas believes it is not accidental that existentialist interpreters like Bultmann have found gnosticism so fascinating. The various gnostic religious movements have become prominent in our society when our needs and suspicions are much the same as those of the society that produced such literature.

may strike as realistic those who have been profoundly shaped by suspicion and what Kermode terms the "unfollowability" of the world. The ending—frightened women too terrified to say anything to anyone—may seem more compelling than conclusions that tie up all the loose ends. Precisely to such a world could a realistic word of promise be spoken. There are good reasons for possibly finding Mark's Gospel attractive, and our encounter with this narrative could offer promise beyond psychological satisfaction. Perhaps "the beginning of the good news of Jesus Christ" is a message capable of awakening tired and impoverished imaginations. This will depend upon the success we have as interpreters making an argument one way or the other. Admittedly, the success of that enterprise remains to be seen.

Part Two

CHALLENGING
PROMISES

3

Transgressing Boundaries: Jesus' Baptism in Mark

The terse report of Jesus' baptism in Mark's Gospel takes up a total of three verses (Mark 1:9-11). When read aloud, the account lasts no more than a few seconds. Yet much happens in these few verses that is important for understanding the character of Mark's story. This brevity is particularly striking in view of how important the scene has been for would-be biographers of Jesus. The information the narrator fails to provide is at least as impressive as what he does. Where is Jesus from, in terms of family, background, education, or anything that would shed light on his preparation for this moment? Why should he come all the way from Nazareth to be baptized by John? How did he understand the baptism? Was the voice from heaven, assuming its reality, something new for Jesus? What did John think of it—or did he see or hear anything? What about the crowds?

The remarkable lack of interest in surface details, as is well known, characterizes much of Mark's Gospel, and it forces some reflection even at this point on the character of his composition as narrative. As is also well known, the lack of detail and the episodic rhythm have led to considerable speculation about sources and the process by which such a work took shape. Some time ago, however, no less a student of narrative than Eric Auerbach insisted on pressing literary questions.[1] Why are these details reported and not others? What kind of a story are we dealing with? Markan scholarship in the last two decades has

---

1. Eric Auerbach, *Mimesis*, trans. W. R. Trask (Princeton, N.J.: Princeton University Press, 1953).

discovered all sorts of interesting things about the Gospel by pressing such questions.

The Tearing of the Heavens

Before we can examine what Mark reports, it is important to get the details straight. Because most Bible readers must rely on translations from the Greek, proper rendering of the language remains a priority. Perhaps that is obvious. Consider, however, the RSV rendering of verse 10—a rendering that determined for a large number of English-speaking Bible readers how the text was heard: "And when he came up out of the water, immediately he saw the heavens opened." While Matthew and Luke use the verb *anoigo*, which means "open," Mark uses *schizo*, which means "tear" or "rip." The phrase *"schizomenous tous ouranous"* can be translated "the heavens opened" only if the translator has Matthew in mind. Something like "and he saw the heavens being torn apart" is demanded. The rendering in the NRSV, "he saw the heavens torn apart," is considerably better, although "torn" still treats the participle as though it denoted a completed action. The Greek suggests something dramatic in the process of taking place.

The importance of an accurate rendering of the Greek is difficult to overestimate. The image in Mark is strong, even violent, and the moment that is noted, the imagination begins to work. If the heavens are opened, then they may well close again. If they are torn apart, however, then we may think of some permanent damage or rupture that cannot be repaired. Further, those who know Mark at all think immediately of the tearing of the temple curtain at the moment of Jesus' death: "And the curtain of the temple was torn in two, from top to bottom" (15:38; the verb is the same, *eschisthe*). The images form an inclusio: A pattern that begins here at Jesus' baptism ends with his death.

The mere use of a term like *inclusio* suggests some literary pattern or design that a reader may observe in the narrative, an approach to the story that earlier generations of Bible readers may not have considered warranted. Further analysis only confirms the hunch that this approach yields some results. When the heavens are torn, the Spirit enters Jesus and a heavenly voice addresses him as "son." At the moment of his death, he "breathed out his spirit" (15:37, au. trans.); the temple curtain tears; and a centurion—not God—makes a declaration about Jesus' sonship. Reflection suggests that the relationship between both ends of the inclusio are complex, not simple, and merit further study.

Perhaps the most intriguing image is the tearing of the heavens and the temple curtain. The lack of interpretive detail—particularly in chapter 15, where the relationship of Jesus' death to the tearing of the curtain and of the tearing to the centurion's declaration are not explained (15:38-39)—suggests that the author trusts the imagination of the readers. This is a far more likely inference than that the author did not understand what he wrote. An appropriate question is thus how imagination is expected to work. Imagination is not given free play; the author does provide some constraints. It may be that some constraint is exercised by shared symbols. Most commentators presume that the tearing of the curtain at Jesus' death has to do with the barrier to the Holy of Holies in the Temple, which provided protection from a dangerous encounter with God, an encounter that meant certain death for human beings.[2] The elimination of a barrier between God and creation, clearest in the tearing of the temple curtain, may be suggested in the baptismal scene as well.

The "curtain" here may also be the one Josephus describes at the entrance to the sanctuary building:

> Before these hung a veil of equal length, of Babylonian tapestry, with embroidery of blue and fine linen, of scarlet also and purple, wrought with marvelous skill. Nor was this mixture of materials without its mystic meaning: it typified the universe. For the scarlet seemed emblematic of fire, the fine linen of the earth, the blue of the air, and the purple of the sea; the comparison in two cases being suggested by their colour, and in that of the fine linen and purple by their origin, as the one is produced by the earth and the other by the sea. On this tapestry was portrayed a panorama of the heavens, the signs of the Zodiac excepted.[3]

A possible connection with the baptismal scene is quite apparent here. The heavens, understood as a great cosmic curtain that separates creation from God's presence, are in the process of being torn open.

What does the tearing mean? It may mean, as interpreted in the Letter to the Hebrews (esp. chapters 9–10), that we now have access to God: We can "have confidence to enter the sanctuary by the blood of Jesus" (Heb. 10:19). Viewed from another perspective, the image may suggest that the protecting barriers are gone and that God, unwilling to be confined to sacred spaces, is on the loose in our own

---

2. The possibility that the reference speaks of another "curtain" that served as the door to the sanctuary in the summer might suggest parallels to Jewish traditions about portents of the destruction of the Second Temple. For a discussion of the data, see Juel, *Messiah and Temple: The Trial of Jesus in the Gospel of Mark*, SBLDS 31 (Missoula, Mont.: Scholars Press, 1977), 140–43.

3. Josephus, *Wars* V, 212–14.

realm. If characters in the story find Jesus' ministry threatening, then they may have good reason.

The imagery has enormous power to shape imagination and to open readers to the story. That is, Mark's narrative is about the intrusion of God into a world that has become alien territory—an intrusion that means both death and life. That the author allows such associations suggests that something holds the story together, but that little explicit help will be given for making the connections. Reading will require imagination and involvement; some information about imagery familiar to author and audience will turn out to be helpful. Interpreting our pericope thus provides clues to the nature of the narrative basic to an appreciation of the story.

The rending of the heavens makes possible further action. The Spirit descends "into" Jesus. That we are to understand the Spirit as inhabiting Jesus is apparent from the dispute in Mark 3:22-30, where the charge that Jesus is possessed by unclean spirits is characterized as blasphemy "against the Holy Spirit." Jesus is possessed—but by God's Spirit.

Confirmation and Anticipation

The rending of the heavens issues in another occurrence: A heavenly voice makes a declaration. The words from heaven provide the climax of the story: "You are my Son, the Beloved; with you I am well pleased." When the words have been spoken (again, without comment by the narrator), the story moves on—without reporting the reaction of any characters in the drama. As with virtually all the declarations of Jesus' sonship, the words are for the benefit of the reader. No characters in the story appear to hear the declarations of the demons (3:11; 5:7). And while at the Transfiguration, the voice declares that "This is my Son . . ." (9:7), including at least the three disciples in the revelation, no indication is given that "Son of God" is a title even the disciples recognize as significant or appropriate.

Upon closer examination, we discover that virtually all the words in the heavenly communication can be found in the Bible of Israel. Perhaps that is only appropriate: God speaks using biblical words and phrases (although, it should be noted, the scriptural words in Mark generally come from the Greek Bible, not the Hebrew). That observation, however, may suggest that the particular words and phrases have further significance. Background becomes potentially important once again as a force that shapes the imagination of the reader.

The first words, "You are my Son," appear to be taken from Psalm 2:7, a psalm that as early as the Qumran Scrolls was understood as an oracle predicting the coming of the Messiah.[4] In the baptismal scene, God declares that Jesus is his Son using words taken from a messianic oracle in which God makes the same declaration. The identity of Jesus, while a secret hidden from most of the characters in the story, is known to the reader: Mark begins with a statement that the story has to do with "Jesus Christ, [the Son of God]."[5] "For those who know the psalm, the association of Jesus with messianic promises appropriately confirms what has been stated by the narrator.

The last words, "with you I am well pleased," are taken from Isaiah 42:1 (although not from the Septuagint rendering). The relevance of these statements about the mysterious servant of the Lord are clear, especially again to those who know the whole verse: "Here is my servant, whom I uphold, my chosen, in whom my soul delights; I have put my spirit upon him; he will bring forth justice to the nations." The words associate Jesus with the unidentified and mysterious servant in Isaiah who has an important role to play in God's future plans.[6]

The reference to a beloved son is suggestive, linking Jesus with another beloved son, Isaac, whose destiny was to be offered as a sacrifice on a mountain (Gen. 22:2). A link between Jesus' baptism and the famous Akedah cannot be determined solely on the basis of Mark 1:11. The currency of Christian use of Genesis 22 needs to be investigated to determine the probability of an allusion here in Mark 1. A study of Jewish interpretive tradition would provide additional support for such a hunch.[7]

The words spoken from heaven obviously have a history that extends behind Mark's Gospel. They come from the Scriptures, and, for those familiar with them, a script for Jesus' ministry emerges. This strange event serves as a confirmation that Jesus is the Messiah, God's Son; the servant on whom God will pour out his Spirit, whose destiny is to bring justice to the nations; and perhaps even the Son who is destined to die.

Scriptural precedent may not be restricted only to clear-cut allusions. Commentators have suggested that Isaiah 64:1 lies behind the account: "O that you would tear open the heavens and come down." The suggestion is worth pursuing, although it is interesting that the Septuagint

4. On the use of this psalm, see Juel, *Messianic Exegesis* (Philadelphia: Fortress Press, 1988), 77–81.

5. Understanding "Son of God" in 1:11 as a messianic designation does not depend upon the variant reading in 1:1 (see 14:61, where "the Son of the Blessed" appears with "the Christ").

6. On the use of "servant" passages from Isaiah, see Juel, *Messianic Exegesis*, chap. 4.

7. Such investigation has, in fact, provided such support. See esp. Nils Dahl, "The Atonement: An Adequate Reward for the Akedah?" in *Jesus the Christ* (Minneapolis: Fortress Press, 1991), 137–52, and the literature there cited.

uses the verb *anoigo* and not *schizo*. That would make the versions of
the story in Matthew and Luke more likely allusions to Isaiah 64, at
least in the Septuagint form. The sense of the verses seems more appropriately captured in Mark, however, where God's presence on this
side of the heavens is a threat as well as a promise. In Isaiah, the tearing
of the heavens and God's coming will mean that mountains will quake
and nations will "tremble at your presence" (Isa. 64:2).

Containing a Scandal

Regardless of the biblical allusions for which we might make a compelling argument, they make sense only to those who know the Bible.
Mark provides no hint that the words should be familiar. The depth of
the story becomes apparent only in light of special information—suggesting that if it is not already obvious Mark writes for a particular
audience, with particular knowledge and competencies.

Formal analysis of the three verses yields little of substance. Classification of the episode as a faith legend (Bultmann) may provide some
information about the early church, but the reconstructed setting within
which to locate such a legend remains largely speculative. More interesting is study of the account in light of intertestamental literature,
specifically the Psalms of Solomon 17, 18, and the Testament of the
Twelve Patriarchs. In the two famous Psalms of Solomon, the Lord's
Anointed is depicted as one on whom God pours out his Spirit (17:42
and 18:8). Even more striking are parallels with the confirmation scenes
in the Testament of Levi 18 and the Testament of Judah 24:1, where
the eschatological priest and the Messiah are respectively confirmed in
a manner reminiscent of Mark 1. In both cases, the heavens open and
the spirit descends on the eschatological priest or the messianic king;
and in the case of the priest, God speaks, says the narrator, "as from
Abraham to Isaac." Separating Christian interpolations in the Testament
of the Twelve from a more ancient text is difficult in these sections, but
it is at least possible that in the narrative of Jesus' baptism the scene
itself—the opening of the heavens, the coming of the Spirit, and a
confirming declaration from God—is traditional. The question is worth
further exploration.

Thus far analysis has been confined to the verses themselves (apart
from the reference to Mark 15). Perhaps the most interesting and important information about the pericope emerges when it is related to
its context. The preceding verses, which speak about John the Baptizer,
are essential to exegesis of 1:9-11. On the one hand, the verses provide

further traditional confirmation that Jesus is the coming one: John the Baptist appears as Elijah in the role of forerunner. John's clothing, mentioned in verse 6, is reminiscent of 2 Kings 1:8 (it is what Elijah wears); the allusion to Malachi 3:1 in Mark 1:2 (incorrectly ascribed only to Isaiah) was traditionally tied to Malachi 4:5-6, which predicts the coming of Elijah. John appears as an eschatological figure. And as forerunner, he points to Jesus, the one who comes after, whose sandal thong he is unworthy to untie. As a symbol of Jesus' superiority, baptism by the Spirit (a higher form of purification than water) is promised in contrast to John's baptism (Mark 1:8). He will do greater things than John.

Yet the force of this preparation by John is equally bound up with his role as a preacher of repentance. His baptism is part of his message of repentance and forgiveness (1:4). Jesus will be known by an even higher order of baptism. But when Jesus arrives on the scene after all the buildup, he does no baptizing; he is baptized. And he submits without explanation to a baptism of repentance for the forgiveness of sins.

The scandal is sensed by Matthew and Luke. In Matthew, the dialogue between John and Jesus acknowledges the problem and provides assurance that Jesus is indeed the superior and that all this is what God intends. "John would have prevented him, saying, 'I need to be baptized by you, and do you come to me?' But Jesus answered him, 'Let it be so now; for it is proper for us in this way to fulfill all righteousness'" (Matt. 3:14-15). In Luke, the report of John's arrest prior to the report of Jesus' baptism psychologically removes John from the scene and blunts the scandal (Luke 3:18-22)

Mark does not seek to blunt the scandal; his narrative creates the problem. Jesus is the one for whom John has prepared and for whom Israel has waited. The tearing of the heavens, the descent of the Spirit, and the heavenly voice confirm that. But Jesus' confirmation is a surprise, a shock; it occurs as part of a baptism of repentance for the forgiveness of sins. The Christ, the Son of God, opens his ministry where he is not expected, with outcasts in some desert place. When the expected one appears, he does not meet expectations. This initial impression, created by the baptismal story, provides the motive power that carries the story forward. This unexpected inauguration of the king on the occasion of his baptism by John leads inexorably to a cross where he will die as "the King of the Jews."

Transgressing Boundaries

The proposal that the account of Jesus' baptism introduces a predominant theme for reading the story requires substantiation. I have chosen to speak of this theme in Mark as "transgressing boundaries." The imagery has been employed by others, which I take to be an indication of its appropriateness. This vantage point is helpful for organizing much of the material in the opening chapters as well as the passion tradition.

Mark's opening chapters are filled with ritual imagery that deals largely with matters of purity. In his first public act, Jesus is confronted by an unclean spirit in a holy place (1:21-28). Jesus drives the spirit out, yet in doing so he initiates a ministry in which he will himself violate ritual boundaries. He acts with unprecedented authority, not like the scribes (1:22, 27). In the scenes that follow, Jesus touches a leper (1:40-45), eats with the unwashed (2:15-17), heals on the Sabbath (3:1-6), even justifies his disciples' plucking grain on the Sabbath (2:23-28). And in his declaration to the paralytic—"Your sins are forgiven" (2:5)—he violates perhaps the most important ritual boundary of all, the one separating God from the created order. The sin that introduces the whole story of salvation in Genesis is the surrender to the temptation to be like God. Jesus presumes to speak and act for God, thus eliciting from onlookers the charge that he commits blasphemy (2:7). The charge of blasphemy will return at Jesus' trial before the Sanhedrin, the story's climax, providing the basis for his condemnation at the hands of the religious authorities.

Appropriately, the characters in the opening chapters who find Jesus most troublesome are Pharisees—observant Jews whose religious conception consists in the construction and maintenance of boundaries between clean and unclean, between the sacred and the profane, between God and the created order. Jacob Neusner offers helpful comments on the ontology of the Pharisees:

> The Pharisaic stress on eating food suitable for the cult and eating it in conditions of cultic cleanness means that, for their system of piety, the central metaphor is the cult, by analogy to which what is clean is deemed clean, and what is unclean, unclean. That analogy is inevitable, given the system's ontological conviction that regularity, permanence, recurrence, and perpetual activity define what is normal and delimit life from non-life. For the ontology in this context is ultimately realized in that permanent, recurrent, and perfect world created by the cult and extending its lines of structure and order from the center which is the cult to the periphery formed by the setting of holy Land and People.[8]

8. Jacob Neusner, "First-Century Pharisaism," *Approaches to Ancient Judaism: Theory and Practice*, ed. Scott Green, Brown Judaic Series 1 (Missoula, Mont.: Scholars Press, 1978), 224.

To such a system Jesus is a threat. Although a religious Jew, he associates with the unwashed and the impious, threatens Sabbath observance, and claims an authority that verges on blasphemy. He begins his career among sinners and tax collectors who have come to John to be washed. His presence among them, and his consistent willingness to move beyond the bounds of propriety, generate criticism that gains momentum as the story progresses.

The argument that the narrative seeks to make, if we may use such language, is that Jesus must transgress the bounds of propriety and tradition for the sake of a higher good. He is rendered unclean neither by his contact with a leper or a demoniac in the land of the Gerasenes nor by contact with an unclean woman or a dead girl (5:21-43). People are cleansed by his touch; lives are restored. For the responsible and pious, however, the price is too great. Religious people know the danger of chaos and prefer to live within the safe domain of the tradition; the law, after all, is the gift of God. Jesus' relatives, knowing his origin, believe him to be mad (3:20-21, contrary to NRSV); the scribes from Jerusalem, who cannot deny his power, attribute it to demonic possession (3:22); the inhabitants of the land of the Gerasenes, when they see the former demoniac clothed and in his right mind, ask Jesus to leave, preferring a world in which the boundaries between clean and unclean are secure (5:17). It becomes inevitable ("the Son of Man must undergo great suffering," as Jesus puts it, in 8:31) that both the religious and political leaders must destroy Jesus as a threat to the tradition, to law and order, and as an affront to common sense. The image of the crucified King of the Jews captures the tensions as well as the ironies of the story. Jesus is the King—the Messiah, the Son of God. He also looks nothing like a king. And it is only in the relationship of the two facts—his identity as Messiah and his appearance as the crucified King of the Jews—that the truth of the story can be expressed.

The terse account of Jesus' baptism introduces us to the truth that will generate a whole story: Jesus is confirmed as Messiah by a heavenly act and declaration—but outside the Holy City and the sanctuary, among the impure who have come for cleansing. His career will shatter expectations throughout, creating a whole new religious alternative (or, to use Neusner's words, "an essentially distinctive and fresh mode of Judaic piety"). "Fresh skins for new wine," Jesus tells his detractors. Lines must be crossed, curtains torn, the heavens themselves rent asunder in the course of the career of one whose coming can be characterized as good news.

Interpretation and Method

As I reflect on the evolution of my reading of these verses in Mark, the crucial observations have to do with reading the verses in their narrative setting. Form-critical study never seemed to provide much interesting information about the verses. And although redaction criticism seemed at first to offer more promise, its investment in separating tradition and redaction never paid off. What the brief account of Jesus' baptism might have meant in some pre-Markan setting remains highly speculative. Perhaps more importantly, meticulous analysis of 1:9-11 will never appreciate the meaning of the account which becomes apparent only in the movement from the opening verses in the Gospel. Without the information that John preaches a baptism of repentance, the contrast necessary for understanding the story and what it seeks to tell us about Jesus' ministry does not exist. Likewise, the link between the tearing of the heavens at the baptism and tearing of the temple curtain at Jesus' death offers greater appreciation of the image and its interpretive power.

Mark's story is richer for the account of Jesus' baptism. The brief episode focuses the tensions in particular images: the king who does not look like a king; the one who will baptize who is baptized; the one in whose ministry God comes frighteningly close. In light of these images, the dynamics of the unfolding drama make sense. We are offered a glimpse of what this good news is about—and what it will cost.

The information that can be amassed about the background of the scene is important because it serves to confirm interpretive hunches: It fills out the contrast drawn between what is expected and what God actually delivers. Information about the scriptural roots of the voice from heaven (that is, allusions to Ps. 2:7, Isa. 42:1, and Gen. 22), the possible place of the scene itself in pre-Christian eschatological tradition (that is, from the Psalms of Solomon, the Testament of Levi and Judah), and the link between John and Elijah, only up the ante: It makes more precise our sense of the conflict that shall drive the narrative. The background information even heightens the sense of scandal that we too quickly pass over because we are captive to some agenda or another.

For that reason, at least, the concrete details are essential. Jesus is identified as that one whom God calls Son—the "Christ" of whom Psalm 2 speaks. It is as Christ—as "King of the Jews"—that Jesus will die. The contrast between expectations and results arises from and focuses on specific historical information. Attention to such specific features of Mark's narrative and to their background in Jewish tradition provides necessary constraints on the imagination of Mark's interpreters.

As I reflect on what allows for lively engagement with passages such as the account of Jesus' baptism, I am continually reminded about the indispensability of imagination. Slavish adherence to one method or another often succeeds in killing the imagination, rendering the results of interpretation sterile and inaccessible. Imagination needs to be subjected to critique; interpretation ought to be responsible to other readers, which is the point of some common agreement about the kinds of arguments that can convince. For several decades, biblical studies have been dominated by source-critical approaches that give the appearance of being scientific and careful. I continue to be surprised, however, by their limited usefulness and their inability to persuade. Narrative and rhetorical methodologies have already borne more fruit. And whereas they themselves will become so complex as to confound most ordinary readers of texts, their advantage is that they share the goal of facilitating engagement with a story. That engagement, hopefully, will remain the goal of interpretation. As my reading of passages like the account of Jesus' baptism has evolved, I am aware of my own need for methodological clarity. It nevertheless strikes me as a definite advantage that in a field where method becomes so sophisticated and esoteric as to lie beyond the ability of any but the professional, it is still possible to lay bare the truth of a text with tools that are quite within reach of any who can read. The results of such work may turn out to be more interesting, more significant, and more convincing than we have come to expect.

4

Sowing Promises:
Truth in Parable Form

The parables of Jesus not surprisingly have generated a large body of interpretation.[1] The vivid stories have the capacity to engage imagination and, as a generation of scholars have sought to demonstrate, shake foundations and change worlds. Whereas medieval exegetes sought to probe beneath the surface of the stories to the realities below, attempting to decipher their encoded messages, current readers are intent upon an appreciative hearing more appropriate to the parable form. Perrin's brief history of scholarship culminates in a new appreciation of the figurative power of the parable:

> Whereas Jülicher had seen it as an instance of moral instruction, Jeremias as an aspect of the message of Jesus as a whole, and the "new hermeneutic" as a sermon preached by Jesus to his contemporaries, the recent American interpretation has attempted to allow the parable to speak for itself. The assumption has been that if we can understand the parable as metaphor, if we can understand the parable as a story, then the metaphor can be the bearer of reality for us, the story can speak directly to us. We are reaching quite deliberately toward what Paul Ricoeur calls a "post-critical naivete" with regard to the text, toward a reading of the text fully appreciative of its *natural* force and potential meaning.[2]

1. Names of those whose work aims at a more appreciative reading of the parables include Amos Wilder, Robert Funk, Norman Perrin, John Dominic Crossan, and Paul Ricoeur, among others. In this chapter, I am indebted to Richard W. Swanson, whose dissertation I supervised on the parables in Mark, "Parables and Promises Not Kept: An Investigation of the Literary Function of the Parable of the Sower in the Gospel of Mark" (Th.D. diss., Luther-Northwestern Seminary, 1991), has been stimulating and enormously instructive.

2. Norman Perrin, *Jesus and the Language of the Kingdom* (Philadelphia: Fortress Press, 1976), 181.

One of the significant questions raised within the history of modern parable scholarship, however, has been what we are to understand as the text. One might well argue that interpretations have become more appreciative only by extracting the parables from their scriptural settings and delimiting what is read. Current church practice is instructive in this regard. The three-year lectionary, prepared by the Consultation on Common Texts and adapted by most mainline churches, which had the express purpose of engendering greater appreciation of the flow of the respective Gospel narratives, deals with the Parable of the Sower only once, in its Matthean form. Readers are offered the alternative of reading either the parable (Matt. 13:3-8) or the parable with its authorized interpretation (Matt. 13:3-8, 18-23). Nowhere is the scriptural form of the parable, which includes Jesus' comments about his reason for choosing this particular form of discourse, even suggested for public reading.

The same bias against the parables' scriptural settings is at work in most studies of the parables since the epoch-making work of Adolf Jülicher: To receive a proper hearing, the parables must be freed from a suffocating history of interpretation within the church. Liberating the parables from their ecclesial context has included extracting them from their setting within the Gospels (early stages in the ecclesial tradition), a task to which Joachim Jeremias devoted himself with considerable skill and energy. In Jeremias's case, the reason is clearly articulated: The only measure of the legitimacy of interpretation, he argued, was the "intention of the author" of the parables. Jesus told the stories, and we can make claims about what they mean only when we know what he meant. The Gospels are nothing more than the source of what he hopes will be the authentic voice of Jesus.

The impact of his work on Bible reading is difficult to overestimate. Suspicion of the Gospels as distorting runs throughout two generations of interpreters, one important aspect of Jeremias's legacy. Parable readers with any critical sense have been persuaded that their task is to recover the real sense of the parable. Mark and his co-evangelists are alleged to have domesticated the suggestive stories Jesus told. The Gospels are studied to identify redactional features so that they may be discounted in the interpretation of the authentic parable. Appropriate settings for reading the parables, so this argument goes, do not include their literary settings.

Where to locate a parable is critical to its interpretation. The meaning of a parable, as well as its truthfulness, is tied to its function as an analogy. We are not obliged to identify the particular farmer and the location of his field to interpret the Parable of the Sower, but we must know on what reality the parable sheds light. And for such matters we are dependent upon the narrative setting. The Parable of the Sower, like the two other extended similes introduced with "The Kingdom of God is as" or "like" (2:26; 2:30-31), serves to shed light on some other reality—in this case the Kingdom of God and its relationship to Jesus' ministry. To be sure, the parable can be meaningful in a wide variety of settings, as commentators have known since the first reading of Mark's Gospel. The analogy of the mustard seed can be employed to speak about faith; the second parable about the automatic action of the soil can be read as a general wisdom saying about patience.[3] Here, however, the parables are given a particular setting on the basis of which we are to interpret them and to evaluate their truthfulness or adequacy as a representation of how things are with respect to the Kingdom of God.

By liberating the parables from their literary setting, modern parable scholarship has done a great disservice to Scripture and to the community of its interpreters. Arguments about a nonbiblical setting within which to read the parables, whether a proposed historical context in Jesus' ministry or a semantic field constructed with selected biblical (and nonbiblical) material, have not managed to discipline interpretation, but in fact have succeeded in relativizing all questions about meaning and truth. If we cannot agree on a common setting within which to interpret the parables—and there is surely no possibility of agreement on Jeremias's proposed historical setting within the ministry of Jesus—interpreters will continue to talk past one another. As was the case with those in a previous century who hoped that by their study of Jesus they would set free a new and productive force in their world, study of the promising analogies of Jesus by parable scholars seems to lead readers ever further into private worlds from which there is no deliverance.

The proposal that I have adopted is this: The first task of interpreters is to understand the parables in their narrative setting. The Scriptures themselves provide the common ground for our conversations; it is they about which Christian traditions make normative claims. The question of the parables' meaning is tied first to their connection with the story Mark tells. And if they are true in some sense, then we shall do best to pose the question with respect to that narrative setting. Even though a range of narrative readings is possible, the imagination has some constraints. If Mark's Gospel is an argument, and if the parables are critical to the formulation of that argument, then the question can be fairly asked, to what extent the story makes its case. Is the Kingdom of

3. Many parents will be familiar with the chapter entitled "Frog Plants a Garden," in the delightful children's book by Arnold Lobel, *Frog and Toad Together* (New York: Harper and Row, 1973).

God like a farmer who throws seed everywhere? Is some basis provided for expecting from Jesus' efforts a glorious harvest that will at least make sense of the failure and waste?

Historical reflection may be helpful in our reading of the parables. Awareness of the history of the church, even of the career of the historical Jesus can provide confidence in a particular reading of the parables in their narrative setting. If, for example, a proposal must presume an outright contradiction between an alleged original meaning in the mouth of Jesus and the use of the parable in Mark, then such a proposal might have less plausibility than one that sees no enormous chasm between Jesus and the New Testament.[4] The place of historical reflection is clearly secondary, however, to the principal task of interpreting the parables within their literary setting.

Seeing and Not Seeing

A determination to read the Parable of the Sower in its narrative setting produces immediate and dramatic results. Jesus' parable must be read as an allegory for which Mark provides an authorized interpretation (4:13-20). The grammatical awkwardness with which the story about batches of seeds is transformed into a story about four kinds of soil has convinced interpreters that the allegorical explanation is both secondary and forced. If we are interested in the parable within its Gospel setting, however, then we will have to read it as an allegory, however much that may offend aesthetic sensibilities.

An even more striking lesson to be learned from the history of parable scholarship is that the first move of interpreters has been to excuse readers from coming to terms with the difficult words that follow Jesus' telling of the parable. In Mark, Jesus offers an explanation for his choice of figurative speech, and these words are particularly troublesome.

> When he was alone, those who were around him along with the twelve asked him about the parables. And he said to them, "To you has been given the secret of the kingdom of God, but for those outside, everything comes in parables; in order that
> 'they may indeed look, but not perceive,
>   and may indeed listen, but not understand;
> so that they may not turn again and be forgiven.' " (Mark 4:10-12)

4. See the arguments by Nils Dahl in his "The Parables of Growth," in *Jesus in the Memory of the Early Church* (Minneapolis: Augsburg Books, 1976), 141–66.

Jeremias's interpretation is typical. He dismisses both the interpretation in verses 13-20 and the saying about "hardening." His arguments with respect to verses 10-12 are particularly striking. The verses, he argues, have had an unsalutary impact on the reading of parables in early Christianity:

> But above all, the "hardening" theory with regard to the parables, as intended to conceal the mystery of the Kingdom of God from outsiders, led to the predominance of the allegorical method of interpretation.[5]

The secondary character of these verses is obvious. Even though they may represent an authentic saying of Jesus, they do not belong originally in this context and thus have nothing to say about the parables. Mark's grouping of parables is, moreover, "artificial"; the movement is implausible; the explanation can be assigned to a "later stage of the tradition" than the parable.[6] Yet Jeremias is not satisfied even with a demonstration of the secondary character of verses 10-12. Jesus' insistence that he tells riddles "in order that" people not see and hear "so that they may not turn again" does not mean what it says; the statement is less offensive than it sounds, Jeremias argues. On the one hand, the *hina* in verse 12 functions as a formula for introducing scriptural material (Isa. 6:9-10). The problem is thus not so much the intent of Jesus as the will of God recorded in the Scriptures. And precisely at this point, Jeremias insists that Mark has misrepresented the purpose of God by mistranslating the Aramaic of the Targumic tradition on which the Greek must depend (a Targumic tradition which, Jeremias must admit, is itself not without ambiguity). With respect to the critical word from Isaiah, "so that they may not" (*mepote*), Jeremias comments:

> In whatever way the Targumist himself may have understood it, rabbinical exegesis took it to mean "unless," as may be gathered from the fact that it regarded the conclusion of Isa. 6:10 absolutely as a promise that God would forgive his people if they repented. The *mepote* of Mark 4:12 is therefore a rendering of the Targumic *dilemma*, and must be rendered unless.[7]

The logic of this extraordinary tour de force has not escaped most interpreters. It is nothing less than a complete refusal to deal with the biblical text. *Mepote* does not mean "unless." What Jeremias demonstrates is the offense of the statement and an inability to hold together

---

5. J. Jeremias, *The Parables of Jesus*, trans. S. H. Hooke (New York: Scribners, 1962), 13.

6. Jeremias, *Parables*, 13.

7. Jeremias, *Parables*, 17.

parable and explanation. When confronted with such a problem, he invents his own text.

The scriptural text has not fared better among Jeremias's successors. No less a scholar than Raymond Brown can still refer to the verses as Mark's parable theory. The presumption is that they are only the perspective of the evangelist and thus have diminished force. It is striking how many modern students of the parables refuse to take the words seriously, finding one excuse or another for dismissing their implications.

Three Proposals

Among recent literature are notable exceptions. Several works have appeared in the last half decade in which scholars wrestle with the parables in their narrative settings. The implication, for these scholars, is that Mark 4:10-12 is part of the scriptural setting and cannot be dismissed.

Vernon Robbins

In his *Jesus the Teacher*, Vernon Robbins undertakes a rhetorical study of Mark's Gospel.[8] In his comments on Mark 4:11-13, Robbins suggests the utility of comparing the exchange between Jesus and his disciples with the dialogue in Plato's *Theaetetus*. The parallels confirm, he argues, what the reader suspects: Jesus, like Socrates, is being ironic.[9] By *irony*, Robbins apparently means a kind of intellectual teasing that lures an audience (here, the readers of Mark) into pursuing questions further. That Jesus cannot mean what he says, Robbins argues, is confirmed by Mark 8:17-18, when the same comments about the inability to see and hear are applied to the disciples. Whereas these enigmatic words surely shock the casual reader to attention and create interest in what follows, most readers have not been clever enough to detect the irony. The allusion to Isaiah 6 does little to lessen the conviction that Jesus' words mean what they say. He intends to confound. That his disclosure of secrets does not open the minds of the disciples surely does not imply that keeping them from others results in enlightenment. Robbins has nicely identified various rhetorical features of the Gospel, but we may ask how adequately he has identified Mark's argument. What does Jesus'

---

8. Vernon Robbins, *Jesus the Teacher: a Socio-Rhetorical Interpretation of Mark* (Philadelphia: Fortress Press, 1984).

9. Robbins, *Teacher*, 138.

intellectual teasing accomplish in the story? The real irony seems to be
that no one sees or hears. Jesus dies in the dark, with a final misunderstanding of his last words by a group of bystanders, and frightened
women saying nothing to anyone.[10]

John Donahue

John Donahue's comments in his *The Gospel as Parable* press the matter
further.[11] He carefully dismisses the scholarly attempts at evasion before
offering comments of his own. He refuses to dismiss the verses as merely
redactional or a later gloss. The matter of earlier and later have no
relevance in a reading of the Gospel as a whole. As part of Mark's story,
the verses are to be taken seriously.

His interpretation has several parts. First, Donahue understands the
"you" and "outsiders" of Mark 4:10-12 as referring to wider groups.
Appealing to the preceding discussion of inside and outside in 3:20-
32, Donahue points out that the crowds are portrayed as insiders whereas Jesus' relatives are outsiders. That, he believes, must qualify the
"insiders" and "outsiders" in 4:10-12:

> I would claim, then, that the distinction between those around Jesus and
> the outsiders is not between called disciples and the crowd, nor is it
> between Jews and Christians, but it is a distinction between those who
> will understand the true meaning of discipleship and those who will not.
> "Inside" and "outside" are existential, religious categories, determined by
> the kind of response one makes to the demands of Jesus. One of the great
> paradoxes in Mark is that Peter, the one first called (1:16-17), who stands
> at the head of the Twelve (3:16), in his final appearance of the Gospel,
> goes "outside," where he denies that he ever knew Jesus (14:68-71).[12]

Donahue argues convincingly that we ought to hear warnings in
Jesus' words to his disciples and in the parable explanation that follows.
Jesus entrusts the mystery to an inside group, while he promises much
failure before the harvest comes. The story details the various sorts of
failure anticipated in the parable, which seem to include even the disciples as examples of rocky soil.

Less clear is where one hears promise in these words. The promise
in the parable, according to Donahue, can only apply to readers of the
Gospel:

> The seed (word) which will bear fruit is that which is heard and accepted
> (4:20). This last verse functions as an example of true discipleship for

---

10. Robbins's consistent interest in formal parallels and patterns in the narrative seems
in this case to have obscured the particulars of the message.

11. John Donahue, *The Gospel in Parable* (Philadelphia: Fortress Press, 1988).

12. Donahue, *Parable*, 44.

the Markan community. The summons to discipleship is in the form of
a call (1:16-20, 2:14-15) and its reward will be "a hundredfold" (10:30),
just as the good seed bears fruit a hundred fold.[13]

Yet we may well ask where the promise lies for the Markan community,
at least as embodied in present readers. If even those to whom Jesus
entrusted the mystery of the Kingdom of God failed, then what gives
confidence for expecting success elsewhere? The story is about repeated
failure, according to Donahue, not success. While he is surely correct
that these parables are about grace, where is this to be found in the
story? The suggestion that somehow readers will respond appropriately
to the offer of grace—while the disciples and everyone else did not—
sounds hollow. The proposal is reminiscent of the host of sermons
preached on the parable that pose the question, What kind of soil are
you? and conclude with the injunction: Be good soil! The parable
includes no imperatives other than Listen! and soil hardly lends itself
as an image for talking about exhortation and change.

Even though Donahue does not shy away from the difficult verses,
he tends to soften Jesus' insistence that he conceals the truth. Donahue
speaks of a prophetic word by which Jesus anticipates failure as well as
success (that would make the *hina* one of result, not purpose) or in
which the church can reflect on the reality of unbelief. The move allows
belief and unbelief to remain in the hands of the hearers and to make
God the responder. Donahue offers a convincing argument for linking
the understanding of parables with the scandal of Jesus' cross. But if
the parables are also linked with Jesus' proclamation of the Kingdom
of God and the demand to "repent, and believe in the good news"
(1:15), if Jesus intentionally excludes outsiders "so that they may not
turn again and be forgiven"[14] (4:12), and if the narrative argument
focuses on the failure even of the disciples to perform, then it is difficult
to see how readers can find promise in these words of Jesus that they
have a better chance of producing.

Mary Ann Tolbert

Mary Ann Tolbert, whose book sets out to offer an interpretation of
the whole of Mark's Gospel in which the Parable of the Sower has a
crucial role, likewise does not dismiss the verses simply because they
may be secondary.[15] As part of the authorized interpretation of the

13. Donahue, *Parable*, 47.
14. Donahue, *Parable*, 46.
15. Mary Ann Tolbert, *Sowing the Gospel: Mark's World in Literary-Historical Perspective*
(Minneapolis: Fortress Press, 1989), 160–61.

parable, they need to be taken seriously by Mark's readers. She also argues that the verses are not as ominous as they sound. Agreeing with Donahue that the verses should be read in light of Mark 3:31-35, she insists that the outsiders cannot be identified with the crowd to whom Jesus is speaking but with "that class of people who, for whatever reason, do *not* do the will of God."[16] "You" includes more than the twelve disciples (4:10), a "considerably larger group."

> Thus the division between those who are given the mystery, the insiders, and those who hear riddles, the outsiders, is not a simple opposition of disciples versus crowds; instead, it is an opposition of categories: those who do the will of God and those who do not, those who have ears to hear and those who have not. The same parable will be heard differently by these two groups, for outsiders *will not* understand, *because they are outsiders*, and insiders *will* understand *because they are insiders*. The parables, like Jesus' healing and preaching ministry in general, do not force people outside or pull people inside; they simply reveal the type of ground already present.[17]

One might well ask how Tolbert can assert that Jesus' parables "do not force people outside or pull people inside," when his words suggest that is precisely their function. She legitimately turns to the rest of the Gospel for a deeper understanding of the harsh words, but it is unclear what she finds. On the one hand, her interpretation seems far more fatalistic than Jesus': One is simply one kind of soil or another, and Jesus only reveals what one is. Further, according to Tolbert the story systematically reveals the utter absence of good soil among the active characters in the story:

> By the time of Jesus' crucifixion and unexpectedly sudden death on the cross, all the active character groups from earlier sections of the story— the Jerusalem authorities, Jesus' neighbors and kin, and the Twelve— have supplied graphic evidence of their failure and basic identity with the various kinds of unfruitful ground. Whatever expectations they may have embodied have now been fully demolished and their *eternal* bad fortune guaranteed.[18]

This fatalism makes it a bit difficult, however, to understand her repeated use of imperatives later in the book. She suggests that the rhetorical effect of the Gospel is to create a perfect disciple:

> By involving the audience in the narrative time of Jesus' life and death, by aligning their evaluative perspective with that of the narrator and

16. Tolbert, *Sowing*, 160.
17. Tolbert, *Sowing*, 160–61.
18. Tolbert, *Sowing*, 290.

Jesus, by permitting them to share superior knowledge from the beginning of who Jesus was and what he was in the world to do, Mark has created in the role of the authorial audience the perfect disciple. . . .

Just as Jesus preached his performative word to the crowds of Galilee, just so does the Gospel of Mark as a whole seek to be a performative word for its audience.[19]

How can one not wince when Tolbert poses the questions raised by the ending of the Gospel:

In the end, Mark's Gospel purposely leaves each reader and hearer with the urgent and disturbing question: What type of earth am I? Will I go and tell? Indeed, one's response to the seed sown by the Gospel of Mark reveals in each listener's heart, as did Jesus' earlier preaching, the presence of God's ground or Satan's.[20]

It is difficult to imagine a word with less promise or a seed less likely to produce. On the one hand, the performative character of Jesus' words is limited to revealing what is already the case; on the other hand, the questions come at the end of a story in which every character is allegedly exposed as unfruitful soil. Where is the action of God here? What possible evidence does the story—as Tolbert reads it—provide that any current reader will bear fruit? More credible are Kafka's parables, in which the promise of getting inside is held up only to set up the disappointment that is the inevitable mark of human experience.

That Tolbert manages to find room for some imperative in her reading of the parables is of little comfort. The invitation to human effort turns out to be nothing more than the mask behind which lies an unyielding fate.

Another Opinion

I wish to suggest another reading of the parable within its narrative setting as an alternative. While a full treatment is impossible, some lines may be sketched that are worth exploring.

The Parable and Its Interpretation

The most obvious feature of the Parable of the Sower is that it is interpreted—a phenomenon seldom encountered in the Synoptic tradition. Even without elaborate theories about transmission of tradition,

19. Tolbert, *Sowing*, 297.
20. Tolbert, *Sowing*, 299.

the secondary nature of the interpretation is obvious. It is purchased at the expense of grammatical clarity. In the parable itself, the narrator focuses on four batches of seed (*ho, ho, allo, alla*). In the interpretation, we are told that the seed represents the Word (singular). The four batches are represented in the interpretation by relative pronouns, but the explanations then proceed to apply the pronouns to the types of soil, the receptors of the seed (thus the title, "the four types of soil").

There is more than one grammatical irregularity. Not only are the plural relative pronouns at odds with the allegory, which reads "seed" as singular (Mark 4:14); they are all masculine pronouns. The four pronouns in the parable are neuter, and if it is true that the allegorical interpretation reads the four "they-groups" as soil, the terms for the receptors of the seed in the original parable are feminine (*hodos, ge*) or neuter (*petrodes*). The only possibility for making sense of the grammar is to understand the relative pronouns as at least indirectly influenced by the *hoi peri autou* and the *ekeinoi* in verses 10-12. That would suggest that the whole unit, 1-20, belongs together in its present setting. However awkward the transitions at verse 10 and verse 13 may appear, 13-20 do not make sense grammatically without the presence of verses 10-12.

In its literary setting, the parable is interpreted in two ways. First, it is identified as enigmatic speech, designed to conceal. Second, it is transformed into an account of four different types of soil—that is, it becomes a story about the reception the seed will receive. How is the little story to be read?

Setting

The context for the parable is provided by the narrative. Since his first appearance at the Jordan for baptism at John's hand, Jesus has turned up where he is not expected. Observant Jews consistently criticize him for his willingness to associate with the unwashed and to transgress the sacred boundaries by which the religious community orders its life. Jesus is dangerous, and Mark makes little effort to disguise the danger. Immediately prior to the parable chapter, he makes a pronouncement about true family, which is an attack on the most fundamental of all social structures (Mark 3:31-35). In view of the impending coming of the Kingdom, the theme of Jesus' preaching, ordinary constraints do not apply. Fasting is inappropriate while the bridegroom is with them (2:18-22); "the Son of Man is lord even of the sabbath" (2:23-28); even blood-relations provide no secure structure in view of the new possibilities attendant on the coming of the Kingdom of God. What matters is doing "the will of God" as it is being performed by the kingdom's agent.

Even though Jesus' family, observant Jews, and the authorities have grave reservations about his ministry, crowds continue to flock to Jesus, and he invests his ministry in a small group of followers he selects. His sovereign summoning of the small band is explained in chapter 3, where they are commissioned (3:13-19).[21] His preaching of the Kingdom, the reason for his coming, results in a group of twelve who will take up his cause and his commission. They will heal and preach—and, we are led to believe, continue his mission when his own ministry is over.

That is the context in which the parables are located. Jesus has invested a great deal in a small band of disciples. One of the questions that runs through the story is the wisdom of this investment: Will it pay dividends? The prospects are not encouraging. The disciples, as we soon learn, show little promise. Their brief success is soon inundated by massive failure and defection.

What of the parable? It seems clear that in Mark, Jesus is identified as the sower. The question the parable implies, if we are to read the figure as a response to a criticism or an implied doubt, has to do not with the certainty of a harvest. The issue, as Nils Dahl points out, is not whether God's Kingdom will one day come but what possible relationship it can have with Jesus' preaching mission.[22] The image of the harvest is familiar from eschatological tradition and can with little difficulty be related to the theme of Jesus' preaching, namely, the coming of God's Kingdom. The parables deal with implied objections to Jesus' preaching: What evidence is there that his efforts have anything to do with the glorious days to come? As with Jesus' preaching so also in the parables, little is offered to inspire confidence in the activity of the farmer. He is careless with his seed, and the prospects of success are threatened at every turn: birds (Satan), poor soil (lack of commitment), weeds (cares and riches). There appears little likelihood that the sower's efforts will prove fruitful. Yet they do—beyond everyone's expectations. The sower, or farmer, knows his business, and once the seed is in the ground the results are sure. The other two seed parables make the same point, with different emphases.

One important feature of the parables is that they employ no imperatives. The harvest cannot be forced or hastened. No injunctions are issued to encourage the soil, a passive image. The parables, all three,

---

21. R. Tannehill, "The Disciples in Mark: The Function of a Narrative Role," JR 57 (1977): 386–405.

22. Dahl, "The Parables of Growth," 155–56.

simply describe how it is with planting, seeds, and soil. The function of the parables is to describe how it is with Jesus—and how it shall be. The parables make promises; obstacles to the harvest will arise, but the harvest shall come. They caution that for a time, little evidence of growth will appear, but that at the proper time, the harvest shall come. They promise that the tiny seed, once sown, shall surely produce a substantial shrub large enough for birds to rest in its shade.

The parables make a considerable difference to the overall narrative, not by motivating action but by offering a brief plot synopsis and a forecast that keeps the reader's attention directed at the road ahead. The story unfolds precisely as the parable promises. Jesus sows seeds lavishly, carelessly. And there is little prospect of a rich harvest. The contrast between his seedy little band and the promised Kingdom of God is glaring. The narrative picks up the imagery and develops it—although not in terms of some clear structure in the Gospel, as though each section of the Gospel represented some stage in the parable. The "cares and riches" become obstacles for at least one character in the story and provide an occasion for Jesus' statement about the danger of wealth (10:24-25)—and a promise about what is nevertheless possible with God. Peter seems as dense as the rocky soil in which plants cannot send down deep roots. The comment about temptation and trials resulting in defection is certainly borne out in the experience of the disciples. The parable, however, promises a harvest. The seed will find root in good soil and will produce. Results shall emerge, even if they are presently concealed.

The implications of these promises for reading the ending of Mark are obvious. The parables introduce momentum into the story that drives beyond the ending into the future when the results of Jesus' planting must begin to emerge. The parables make no demands, only promises that must be borne out in the narrative—if, that is, the parables prove to be "true."

Seeing and Not Perceiving

Even though the Parable of the Sower may have played a particular role in the historical ministry of Jesus, its role in the narrative has to do almost exclusively with readers and not the narrative audience. Jesus' troubling comments about insiders and outsiders, about seeing and not seeing, make sense only to the reader in this larger context. They emphasize what has already been amply embodied in the narrative: Some are inside the circle and others, outside. Further, the insiders have been chosen by Jesus. With the inception of his preaching of the Kingdom comes a series of calls, beginning with Peter, Andrew, James, and John, that leads to his creation of a group of twelve (3:13-19). That a distinction between the Twelve and a larger entourage ("those about him with the twelve"; 4:10) should be reinforced is to be expected; that he explains things to the insiders and not to others is hardly surprising.

What is striking, however, is the contrast between the popular form of the parables and Jesus' expressed intent to conceal. Although the term can mean "dark saying" or "riddle," most of Jesus' parables seem quite simple and clear. Precisely in what sense the parables obscure Jesus' preaching of the Kingdom is itself unclear. Yet the chapter emphasizes that the disciples do not understand what Jesus means and require explanations. And as the story will make clearer, even explanations do not seem to penetrate the imaginations of the disciples. What seems obvious to us is not obvious to Jesus' audience—not even to the disciples, who benefit from commentary outsiders do not receive.

Equally striking is that the lack of insight seems to be precisely what Jesus intends—or perhaps better, what God intends. Perhaps Jeremias is correct that the *hina* marks the words about seeing and not seeing as scriptural. That simply adds depth to them. Jesus does what he does, with the attendant effects, as God's will. Seeing and not seeing, hearing and not hearing are God's business. That is the point of God's words to Isaiah, and the point is the same in Mark. Without seeing and hearing, no repentance shall occur; and without some act of God, no seeing and hearing shall occur. Some of the uneasiness among commentators may be occasioned by the clarity of the theological statement rather than by its obscurity.

We are told in Mark 4:21-22 that this apparent strategy of concealment will not be permanent; lamps are meant to illumine. Nothing is hidden except to be revealed. A thrust in the story moves it not only from planting to harvest but also from concealment to uncovering. Jesus speaks about such matters as well when he instructs the inner circle of the disciples not to speak about the Transfiguration "until after the Son of Man had risen from the dead" (9:9), or when he promises that "the good news must be proclaimed to all the nations" (13:10), or when he points to the time when all will see "the Son of Man coming in clouds" (13:26). Injunctions to silence, addressed to demons and many whom Jesus heals, are caught up in a movement that drives toward eventual revelation and discovery.

Just as the growth of seeds and harvests depend, however, upon forces beyond the control of farmers or soil so also revelation and discovery depend upon some outside force. Following Jesus requires seeing and hearing: "Let anyone with ears to hear listen" (4:23). The problem is that outsiders are not given the possibility of hearing at this point—and even the disciples, who are given the secret and are offered explanations, display a marked obduracy. Even they do not seem to understand. Their hearts appear to have been hardened (6:52; 8:17); like outsiders, they have eyes and ears but can neither see nor hear (8:18).

The question that arises from Mark 4:10-12 is thus even more troubling than at first glance. It seems unfair to withhold insight from outsiders so as to prevent repentance; it seems far more cruel to open the prospect of insight for insiders only to demonstrate that no way is available for the blind and deaf to heal themselves, no means by which those whose hearts have been hardened can engineer their escape. The words can be heard as good news, but only if concealment does not last forever, only if something is able to penetrate the world of darkness and silence in which both insiders and outsiders seem enveloped. If the parables create momentum within the story, Jesus' words about secrets and concealment provide a criterion by which the future will be evaluated: Can God be trusted with the power to conceal and reveal? Are Jesus' words good news or only offensive?

Implications for Reading the Parable

When the Parable of the Sower is read within its narrative context, what is apparent—as Mary Ann Tolbert has observed—is how crucial the narrative setting is for a reading of the parable and how critical the parable becomes as an interpretation of the narrative.

First, the parable needs to be read as speaking about the Kingdom of God. It is, after all, God's work that the parable—and the Gospel— seek to understand. Demons, disciples, crowds, the pious, and the authorities are all affected by the work of God occurring through Jesus' ministry. Appropriately, nature itself provides a vehicle for interpreting the work of the Creator.

Second, the parable is interpreted as having to do with reception of the Word. Whereas the disciples (and their successors) are called to be sowers, they are first receptors. The interpretation of the parable in Mark 4:13-20, and the difficult verses 10-12, are more interested in reception than in the activity of planting. The concluding image of a great harvest has a different force when the problem in view is a fruitful reception of the seed. Both the opening image and the interpretation promise that Jesus' wisdom will be vindicated. But who will provide that vindication by producing fruit? The matter concentrates attention on the disciples who have been given the secret of the Kingdom of God and have been commissioned to become sowers themselves. The issue to which the parable is directed is thus not simply the lack of signs that there has been any germination. The surprise in the story is that the disciples do not obviously begin to produce at all. When so much is invested in the creation of an inner circle who are categorized as the chosen (Jesus' true family), and when the subsequent narrative will detail their almost complete failure to learn and their eventual collapse, one might well ask about the adequacy of the parable. Even though a harvest may come sometime, who will qualify as "good soil" is not at all clear. On what basis, then, can we read the parable as true?

The problem is not as simple as some interpreters have proposed. Some suggest that the promise is made to readers, true insiders who are invited to perform in ways the disciples could not. Such an interpretation must face substantial difficulties, however. The parables offer no opportunity for effort on the part of the soil, a passive metaphor. The absurdity of telling people to be good soil is as apparent as a farmer's addressing unproductive areas in the field with injunctions to produce. Producing is determined by conditions over which soil has little control. To say that the harvest depends upon the promises of God is to say it does not depend upon human efforts. The scandal of this reading becomes apparent the more one tries to force entry into the story. The promise will be apparent to those who know the fruitlessness of trying to be receptive.

More persuasive than such heroic readings of the parable is the interpretation of veteran readers of texts, Meier Sternberg and Frank Kermode. The contempt with which Sternberg regards precisely this aspect of Mark—and of the New Testament as a whole—is crucial evidence that some readers find the story alienating. The narrative seems to resist such exhortative readings:

> Critics have always been exercised about this contrast drawn by Jesus in favor of his disciples, and Frank Kermode has explored it as a paradigm for reading in general. "In all works of interpretation," says Kermode, "there are insiders and outsiders, the former having, or professing to have, immediate access to the mystery, the latter randomly scattered across space and time, and excluded from the elect who mistrust or despise their unauthorized divinizations." However true of the gospels and various later counterparts, I believe, this forms only one of the paradigms of communication or "interpretation" envisaged by literary works, even of the more enigmatic sort; and it is certainly not the Bible's rule.[23]

23. Meier Sternberg, *The Poetics of Biblical Narrative: Ideological Literature and the Drama of Reading,* Indiana Literary Biblical Series (Bloomington, Ind.: Indiana Univ. Press, 1985), 48–49.

In an imaginative comparison of Deuteronomy 30:11-14 and Mark 4:10-12, Sternberg identifies what he believes to be a chasm dividing narrative strategy in the Hebrew Scriptures and in the New Testament:

> The gulf dividing these key statements—one addressed to the Twelve far from the crowd, the other to a whole people for all time [Deut. 30:11-14; 31:11-12]—epitomizes the mutual incompatibility between two ideologies and between two narrative procedures. The Bible has many secrets but no Secret, many levels of interpretation but all equally accessible, so "very near thee" that, given the will, "thou canst do it." By an unintentional yet deeply revealing irony, Jesus in Mark had just been propounding his parables from a boat on the sea to a crowd on the shore. Nothing is more alien to the spirit of biblical narrative than discourse fashioned or meaning hidden across the sea, than speaking in riddles, than the distinction between spiritual insiders and carnal outsiders, than the very idea that anyone with the least claim to inclusion . . . may suffer exclusion.[24]

Frank Kermode presses the point one step further: Even the notion of insiders turns out to be a disappointing fiction. Regardless of what the author may have intended, the narrative succeeds only in making it impossible for readers to become insiders. It generates not secrets capable of being unveiled, but secrecy, impenetrable, unknowable, unfollowable. More honest are Franz Kafka's parables that mock the desire to intrude into the inner sanctum, that force readers to come face to face with the knowledge that even if there is an inside, they will never be admitted.[25]

One of Kermode's great gifts is the ability to unmask interpretive strategies that seek to protect readers against overly difficult and painful insight. He is able to demonstrate the degree to which much scholarship is little more than a way of protecting ourselves from painful or disappointing readings by the employment of cunning and violence. It is difficult to understand in any other light Jeremias's proposal that the problem in Mark 4:12 is a mistranslation of an Aramaic rendering of Isaiah 6. He simply refuses to deal with the text of Scripture, finding refuge in an earlier stage of tradition or in the intention of Jesus. Those who speak of the verses as Mark's parable theory seem little different. Apparently an author's theory need not be taken seriously as the Word of God. It may be an overstatement that almost all contemporary study of Mark 4 is an attempt to rein in a narrative too difficult to control— but if overstated, it is not far off the mark.

24. Sternberg, *Poetics*, 48–49.

25. See esp. the last chapter in Frank Kermode, *The Genesis of Secrecy: On the Interpretation of Narrative* (Cambridge: Harvard Univ. Press, 1979), and the extended discussion of his interpretation in Juel, "The Matter of the Ending," chap. 8 in this volume.

If we must read the whole story, then enough scandals arise for all. Jesus presumes the right, on God's behalf, to determine who sees and who does not. Does the story offer promise of insight to the reader, to any particular reader? Viewing the words as a challenge to be good soil or to perform more adequately than the disciples represents the kind of interpretive self-protection a close reading ought to challenge. But then what are the prospects of any reading—or reader—of the Gospel?

The question is tied to the prospects that lie ahead for Jesus and for his movement. The parables both play on the distinction between insider and outsider, which the narrative has already constructed (chap. 3), and promise its resolution. Secrecy will not be forever (4:21-24); it must be some kind of strategy. Jesus' ministry has a direction, a telos. As the story unfolds, the signs of growth are few, and the signs of failure are many. The parables predicted as much. But when will the germination become visible? When will "all see"? And in view of the direction and momentum generated by the parables, how are we to read the ending in which the hopes of everyone are apparently disappointed?

It would seem reasonable to surmise that the resolution of the major narrative tensions will not be left in the hands of the reader. Kermode is surely correct that the narrative undermines certain readings. Invited inside, readers are not afforded the means of establishing that status: No secret formulae need to be memorized, no hermeneutical keys to be discovered. At the end, Jesus is appropriately absent. No guarantee is given that even readers can have him, no reason for confidence that anyone will perform in such a way as to ensure his coming. Only the unsettling testimony is heard that he is out of the tomb, on the loose— and that he intends to keep the host of promises still awaiting fulfillment at the Gospel's end.

The Gospel narrative is itself dramatic evidence that silence is not the end of things and that the field may yet produce. The story gives reason to trust that Jesus' words will bear fruit. The trustworthiness of his promises is a major theme in the story. His predictions of his own death are fulfilled. His prediction of the disciples' flight and Peter's denial are fulfilled to the letter. His promised resurrection is at least attested by an empty tomb and the words of the young man clothed in white. Some reason is given to believe Jesus' response to Peter that "there is no one who has left house or brothers or sisters . . . who will not receive a hundredfold now in this age—houses, brothers and sisters . . ." (10:28-30); we are to expect the fulfillment of his promise to James and John that "the cup that I drink you will drink; and with the baptism with which I am baptized, you will be baptized" (10:39). It is right to imagine that his parable of the absent householder and his servants in

13:33-37 speaks of the future of his chosen band. And we are surely to expect that his promise to meet his followers in Galilee shall be determined by the same necessity as marked their flight and Peter's denial (14:28-30). It would not be incorrect to say that if the germination and eventual harvest do not include those followers of Jesus in whom the narrative has such an investment, we have no right to regard the parables as true and certainly no reason to hear them as good news.

The narrative offers sufficient reason for such confidence—although without the slightest suggestion that reclamation lies within the realm of human effort. Whatever promise must be at the expense of any confidence in human ability to bring on the harvest. Hope is at hand only because "for God all things are possible" (10:27).

How God works the impossible is even suggested. Not insignificant is how much emphasis is placed on speaking. The gospel shall be proclaimed to all nations, Jesus promises (13:10). The last scene features a speaker of promises in the empty tomb who reminds the women (and readers) of what Jesus has promised: "As he told you" (16:7). The problems to which the parables open us shall be resolved neither by an act of will nor by a more insightful reading. The seed must continually be sown, and final resolution of the drama of planting and harvest will depend upon some future act that will bring the efforts to fruition— to use Mark's language, the return of one on the clouds of heaven. In the meantime, the problems will yield only to a word, spoken from beyond the story and beyond our experience—a word from the one who alone can declare us insiders, establish the truth of the parables and make of them good news.

5

Plundering Satan's Household: Demons and Discipleship

One of the most engaging stories in Mark's Gospel is the account of Jesus' struggle with demons in the region of the Gerasenes. It is also one of the least appreciated because it does not appear in any of the major lectionaries. Many have thus never heard the story. Like the mysterious middle verses in the Parable of the Sower (Mark 4:10-12), this victim of the lectionary system provides surprises and raises expectations for readers of Mark's Gospel. Critical aspects of interpretation include attention to the place of this story within the larger narrative.

Following Jesus' stilling the storm (4:35-41), the account introduces a series of three dramatic miracles that provide a challenging response to the disciples' question, "Who then is this, that even the wind and the sea obey him?" Jesus, we learn, is one who can cast out a legion of unclean spirits, heal a woman of her twelve-year disease (which has rendered her unfit for human society, confounded physicians, and cost her all she had), and even raise a twelve-year-old girl from the dead.

The story, however, does more than report data. Terse summaries in Mark provide reports of Jesus' exorcisms (1:34; 3:11). This lengthy account of Jesus' confrontation with a legion of devils (5:1-20) provides a fuller experience than what summaries typically report. Perhaps the most notable feature of the pericope is the abundance of detail. Mark uses far more words to tell the story of the demoniac than Matthew or Luke. His love of detail reveals a relish for the dramatic perhaps unmatched in the New Testament. Details, at times seemingly redundant, heighten the drama by impressing the audience with the severity of the problem. The man Jesus encounters suffers from no ordinary possession.

Townspeople, in their efforts to subdue him, have tried everything. They have bound the demoniac hand and foot (5:3-4). The narrator dutifully reports: "The chains he wrenched apart, and the shackles he broke in pieces" (5:4). Little wonder no one was able to bind the man, a detail mentioned twice (5:3,4). Two times the author notes that the poor wretch lived among the tombs (5:2,3), adding, "Night and day among the tombs and on the mountains he was always howling and bruising himself with stones" (5:5). The situation is desperate. The signs of possession are painfully obvious to everyone.[1] The man is totally out of control and incapable of living within society. Symbolic of his expulsion from human fellowship, he lives beyond the boundaries of civilization, in a state of ritual uncleanness (from a Jewish perspective), among the dead. Symbols of anti-social behavior extend even to clothing; the demoniac is obviously naked because we are told after the encounter that when the townspeople come to see what has occurred, they find him "sitting there, clothed and in his right mind" (5:15). We ought not miss the significance of comments about apparel, as in the description of John the Baptist (1:6), the young man who flees the guards at Jesus' arrest (14:52), and the young man at the tomb (16:5).

The narrator seems particularly interested in the status of the demoniac as an outsider, making much of the boundaries imagery. The man, he tells us, is possessed by an "unclean spirit" (5:2) or "unclean spirits" (5:13). The land itself is unclean, at least for Jews; pigs graze there; it is a place for the dead, not the living. Cure entails not simply freedom from the demons but also cleansing, which makes possible restoration to normal social life (a return to the village, clothed and in control).

The story recapitulates a familiar theme in Mark: the restoration of an outsider to life within the community, which those in charge of maintaining the boundaries find disquieting. Measured by ordinary social and religious standards, Jesus resists classification as an insider or outsider, which frustrates and bewilders observant Jews. Although obviously religious, he constantly transgresses boundaries: He heals on the Sabbath (1:21-31; 3:1-6); his followers do not fast, as do other observant Jews (2:18-22); Jesus' disciples harvest food on the Sabbath

1. It is instructive to compare the "diagnosis" of possession with the one found in Philostratus' *Life of Apollonius* IV, 20, where anti-social behavior and strange apparel provide decisive evidence. In Philostratus, however, it is the rude and coarse laughter during Apollonius's discourse on libations, singing to himself, and "dainty dress and summery clothing" that betray the presence of a demon in a young man. Most notable is the difference in social strata that distinguishes Mark's account from that of Philostratus.

(2:23-28); he does not instruct his disciples to wash properly before eating (7:1-23); he eats with sinners and tax collectors (2:15-18), and touches lepers (1:41). In the two stories that follow our text, Jesus is touched by an unclean woman with a hemorrhage and takes a dead child by the hand, risking defilement in both cases. In each instance, Jesus transgresses recognized boundaries for the sake of something greater. His association with outcasts and the ritually impure, further-more, results not in his defilement, but in their restoration and cleansing. In various ways, he brings outcasts back into the family. Such behavior follows his stated intention: "Those who are well have no need of a physician, but those who are sick; I have come to call not the righteous but sinners" (2:17). If traditionalists cannot accommodate such behavior within accepted forms, then new forms will have to be created: fresh wineskins for new wine, as Jesus says (2:22). And that is precisely the problem for those who know the importance of boundaries and tra-dition. Jesus acts with an authority that is not subject to traditional standards ("not as the scribes" [1:22]), and no guarantees are available that he will not bring the whole social and religious structure crashing down about him.

The healing of the demoniac belongs with such boundary stories. The variation in narrative audience—we must presume the villagers are Gentiles because they live on "the other side of the sea" and raise pigs—provides a glimpse of how Jesus' ministry will play to a non-Jewish crowd. Still, the narrator describes the whole scene from a Jewish point of view, and the implied audience, the readers for whom Mark tells the story, are presumed to view the action from the same perspective: They are expected to empathize with the Jewish distaste for swine. Mark's readers know that setting foot on such defiled soil is bad enough. Yet readers recognize that even from the perspective of Gentiles, Jesus is transgressing boundaries. The demoniac is an outsider to Gentile out-siders. His superhuman strength and antisocial behavior mark him as possessed; he must live as an outcast, among the dead. And Jesus' healing of the dangerous outsider, suiting him again for life within society, makes the villagers every bit as uncomfortable as the Pharisees and scribes. Although unable to overcome the unclean spirits, the villagers are at least able to draw and maintain boundaries for self-protection. Jesus disrupts their ordered world. His own power, greater than that of the legion, is no more subject to their control than that of the demons, who at least know their place. When they observe what has occurred, when they see the demoniac "sitting there, clothed and in his right mind," the townspeople are not converted. They are "afraid." Their request that Jesus leave the region seems motivated less by anger at the loss of their herd of swine than by their uneasiness about Jesus. He does not fit their experience; he is a challenge to their world. Rather than change, they ask him to leave. Only the former demoniac responds to Jesus' call—appropriately, because he is one of the sick to whom Jesus was sent.

The man's request to accompany Jesus and Jesus' injunction to return home, as well as the narrator's comment that people were astonished at the former demoniac's testimony, are unparalleled in Mark. More often Jesus commands people to say nothing about what has happened to them. That is the case in the story of Jesus' raising of Jairus' daughter a bit later in the narrative (5:43). Whether or not the unique request and response are related to Jesus' presence in Gentile territory must remain an open question.[2] Interestingly the story presumes that word about Jesus has spread among Gentiles. The Greek Syrophoenician woman who comes to ask Jesus' help has obviously heard something about him (7:24-37), as have those who bring to Jesus a man who is deaf and had an impediment in his speech (7:31-37).

The story of the demoniac in the land of the Gerasenes is a dramatic version of a familiar Markan theme. The Jesus of Mark is first of all an exorcist and a healer. Certain elements are common to most of the exorcisms. Here, as in the opening scene in Jesus' public ministry (1:21-28), the demons know Jesus; they recognize him to be "the Holy One of God" (1:24) or "Son of the Most High God" (5:7). The narrator, in an important summary, reports that demons generally recognized Jesus as "the Son of God" (3:11; see also 1:34). Only in Jesus' exorcism of a demon who keeps a boy from speaking and hearing is the recognition motif absent (9:14-29).

The confessions of the demons are intriguing because they appear to have no impact on characters in the story. No one, not even Jesus' disciples, suggests that Jesus is the Son of God (6:14-16; 8:28-30) until the high priest puts the decisive question to Jesus at his trial (14:61). No one seems to hear what the demons shout. The confessions do, however, have an impact on readers. They confirm what we have known from the outset: Jesus is the Christ, the Son of God (1:1). Confirmations

2. W. Kelber, in *Mark's Story of Jesus* (Philadelphia: Fortress Press, 1979), proposes an elaborate structure for the opening chapters in Mark in which crossings of the Sea of Galilee signal respective ministries in Jewish and Gentile territory. The exorcism at the synagogue in Capernaum formally opens the ministry to Jews, the story of the Gerasene demoniac the ministry to Gentiles (pp. 30–33). While the proposal has a bearing on our interpretation of Jesus' unusual response, the confusing geographical data in chaps. 5–8 probably do not permit such neat structuring. The reason for the injunction to tell "how much the Lord has done for you" remains unclear.

come from supernatural beings, from God (1:11 and 9:7) and demons. The confessions emphasize something we know and in doing so exaggerate the distance between the reader and the characters in the story. Somehow the characters cannot grasp what we know to be true.

That distance between the reader and participants in the drama also provides opportunity for irony. The demoniacs' confessions make possible a particular instance of Markan irony. In Mark 3:22-31, Jesus encounters for the first time "scribes who came down from Jerusalem," foreshadowing the climactic confrontation that will occur later. In their opinion, Jesus' ability to cast out demons can only derive from an alliance with the prince of demons. Jesus, they insist, is himself possessed. Their view, of course, is absurd, as Jesus points out in his illustration about kingdoms: Armies do not fight against themselves. If demons are on the run, then it must be because a stronger one has come to tie up the strong man and plunder his house (3:27). The scribes' opinion about Jesus is not without foundation: Jesus is possessed, but by the Spirit of God (note 1:10: the Spirit descends "into" Jesus). Their ascription of Jesus' powers to possession, while close to the truth, nevertheless represents a fatal error: Their conviction that Jesus is in league with the prince of demons represents nothing less than blasphemy against the Holy Spirit, the one sin for which one receives no forgiveness (3:29-30). The irony in the scribes' assessment is that even the demons know better: The demons are only too aware of Jesus' identity, and they know that his arrival marks their end (1:24 and 5:7). The irony is generated by the narrator's report of the confessions of the demoniacs. As readers, we know what only God and the demons know, a truth hidden from the scribes, and, in fact, from everyone else in the story.

The notable absence of an injunction to silence is not the only distinctive feature of the story of the demoniac. The dynamics of this story are unique, particularly the extended dialogue between Jesus and the demoniac. The dialogue may reflect popular beliefs about demons, that is, the importance of learning the demon's name in order to gain power over it. The demon's boasting that its name is "Legion; for we are many" may offer a rather transparent comment on Roman occupation forces, adding a touch of local color.[3] Likewise the destruction of the swine (possessed by the demons) would strike a Jewish audience as a marvelously appropriate ending: Unclean spirits are cleansed in the water, and the vehicles of their destruction are unclean animals.

---

3. The irony may even be more pronounced. The emblem of the legion assigned to Judea was the boar—a wild pig. That fact would make the destruction of the herd of swine all the more entertaining.

Such features suggest that the story is to be enjoyed as much as understood. Jesus' dialogue with the demons does not suggest lack of power as much as it provides an occasion for play. The boast of "Legion" is their undoing; they reveal their name, and with that they are caught. The negotiations about finding another suitable habitat provide an occasion for irony and humor: The demons choose the agency of their own undoing—unclean animals. As suggested above, while the narrative audience is understood as Gentile, in this instance swineherds and towns-people, the story is told for readers—the implied audience—who share Jewish views. We are expected to know about ritual defilement, about tombs, and Gentile territory, and swine. The story presumes readers who share such biases. Discomfort with the story among readers may signal a cultural distance, a matter to which interpretation must attend.[4] Those who are troubled by the loss of property in the story reveal an inability to hear as Jews would hear—and in some cases a significant bias in favor of property rights over human life. Noteworthy is that even the townspeople do not make too much about the loss of personal property. They are more struck by what has occurred to the demoniac.

The secrecy theme, so common in Mark, is conspicuous here by its absence. The cured demoniac is sent home to tell others what has happened to him. We are not told why speaking instead of silence is appropriate here, just as we are not told why other demons, disciples, and others Jesus heals must be silent. We do learn, as we recall, that silence will not last forever: Nothing is hidden, says Jesus, except to be disclosed (4:21-22). The disciples will be able to speak after Jesus has been raised from the dead (9:9). The gospel will be proclaimed to all the nations (13:10). For some reason not stated, heralding can begin here, while in other places Jesus enjoins silence. The deepest irony nevertheless remains: When the time has come to share the news—at another burial place—those commanded to speak are silent: they say nothing to anyone, for they are afraid.

Demons and Disciples

Mark's story focuses more than any of the other Gospels on the interplay between Jesus and his disciples. Unlike the author of the Fourth Gospel,

4. It is not just Westerners who have difficulty with the destruction of the pigs. Chinese readers likewise express puzzlement about the dispensability of swine. In their culture, swine are known to be intelligent animals and can symbolize wisdom. In this case, as others, the distance between the implied audience and the actual audience requires attention. On this, see "The Markan Audience," chap. 9 in this volume.

Mark is more interested in the disciples' performance than that of Jesus'
enemies. In his two articles on Mark, Robert Tannehill has demonstrated
the intertwining of the careers of Jesus and his disciples and the importance of that interplay in the development of the plot.[5] The link
between this pericope and the relationship between master and disciples
so central to the story needs further examination.

The healing of the demoniac provides dramatic evidence of Jesus'
power. That event offers some insight, perhaps, into the meaning of
the titles "Christ, Son of God" with which the Gospel opens, although
the connection with traditional Jewish conceptions is by no means
obvious. This exorcism, with others, is one facet of a complex ministry
that opens with an announcement: The Kingdom of God is at hand.
Jesus' commission from God appears to include healing and exorcism
as well as the task of heralding the impending Kingdom. A direct link
is thus forged between exorcisms and the Kingdom of God. In his
conflict with the Jerusalem scribes, Jesus counters the charge that his
power results from demonic possession and offers his own interpretation
of what his power implies:

> How can Satan cast out Satan? If a kingdom is divided against itself, that
> kingdom cannot stand. And if a house is divided against itself, that house
> will not be able to stand. . . . But no one can enter a strong man's house
> and plunder his property without first tying up the strong man; then
> indeed the house can be plundered. (3:23-27)

Jesus intends to plunder Satan's house—or the house that Satan and
his forces presently occupy. Exorcisms are evidence that Jesus has begun
to seize control, that he has begun to bind the strong one. In the
passage, Jesus parallels "kingdom" and "house." The imagery is suggestive. It appears again at the conclusion of Jesus' farewell discourse
in chapter 13.

> Beware, keep alert; for you do not know when the time will come. It is
> like a man going on a journey, when he leaves home [Greek: "his house-
> hold"] and puts his slaves in charge, each with his work, and commands
> the doorkeeper to be on watch. Therefore, keep awake—for you do not
> know when the *master of the house* will come . . . or else he may find you
> asleep when he comes suddenly. (13:33-36; italics mine)

In almost allegorical fashion, Jesus describes himself as the lord of
the house who leaves his servants in charge. This is not the only occasion

---

5. The two essays by Robert Tannehill are, "The Disciples in Mark: The Function of
a Narrative Role," *Journal of Religion* 57 (1977): 386–405, and "The Gospel of Mark
as Narrative Christology," *Semeia* 16 (1979): 57–95.

on which building imagery is employed to speak of the community of those gathered around Jesus. Later, the church will be described as a "temple not made with hands."[6] It is possible not only to link the Kingdom Jesus heralds with the house he intends to rule; we may perhaps link Jesus' role as Christ, Son of God (= king; see the whole trial and death sequence) with his role as lord of the house. Jesus is not simply the herald of the coming rule of God; he initiates that reign by securing control of the house, establishing a sphere of God's rule. By casting out demons, Jesus fulfills his commission from God—a commission he shares with his disciples (3:13-15). Our story offers perhaps the most dramatic demonstration of Jesus' success in seizing control from Satan: his "legions" are driven into the sea.

Mark takes great pains to link the careers of Jesus' disciples with that of their master. The twelve are chosen as "apostles," emissaries who will, like Jesus, preach and cast out demons (3:14-15). The author is equally scrupulous to distinguish the disciples from others. Following their call, Mark offers contrasting responses by family and religious authorities. While Jesus' disciples have left everything to follow him, his relatives believe he is out of his mind (3:20-21); the scribes insist he is possessed (an assessment that constitutes blasphemy—3:22, 28-30). Even Jesus' mother and brothers seek to whisk Jesus away from the crowds back to his home (3:31). Their efforts occasion a statement about true family: "And looking at those who sat around him, he said, 'Here are my mother and my brothers! Whoever does the will of God is my brother and sister and mother' " (3:34-35).

We cannot help but think of the disciples, those ready to follow at his invitation. The author confirms such inclinations in what follows. The circle imagery ("a crowd was sitting around him," [3:32]; and "looking at those who sat around him" [3:34]) is hardened into categories of "insiders" and "outsiders, "outside" in 3:31, 32). The disciples are insiders to whom "the secret of the kingdom of God" has been given (4:11); while outsiders get riddles (4:11-12), the disciples receive explanations (4:13-20, 34). Yet these concerted efforts to draw clear-cut lines between disciples and outsiders are purposefully undermined at the conclusion of chapter 4 by the first of the three boat scenes in which the disciples reveal a remarkable lack of perception. When Jesus calms the storm, they "were filled with great fear" (4:41, RSV) and ask one another, "Who then is this . . . ?"

The dramatic stories that follow—the Gerasene demoniac, Jairus's daughter, and the woman with a hemorrhage—offer a clear response

___

6. On this see Juel, *Messiah and Temple: The Trial of Jesus in the Gospel of Mark* (Missoula, Mont.: Scholars Press, 1977).

to the disciples' question. Jesus is the "Son of the Most High God," a being with unimaginable power who can drive out legions of demons and can even raise the dead. The spectacular nature of these miracles only heightens our bewilderment at the disciples' continuing incomprehension later (6:45-52). The fear and suspicion of villagers in pagan territory is perhaps understandable (5:16-17); the disbelief of hometown folks in Nazareth has some precedent (6:4-6). Yet after witnessing such spectacles, after performing exorcisms themselves (6:7-13), after eating food miraculously provided by Jesus in the desert (6:30-44), the disciples ought to react with greater insight, but they do not. Their utter amazement at Jesus' second wonder on the sea even elicits from the narrator the comment that their hearts were hardened (6:51-52), a comment picked up in the last of the boat scenes: "Why are you talking about having no bread? Do you still not perceive or understand? Are your hearts hardened? Do you have eyes, and fail to see? Do you have ears, and fail to hear?" (8:17-18).

By depicting Jesus as a man with extraordinary power, fitting out stories with details calculated to elicit amazement from the reader as well as from the crowds, the author drives a wedge between the reader and the disciples. As insiders, as true family, the disciples are certainly the most attractive characters in the story apart from Jesus; in fact, they are the only other real characters. If the reader were to identify with participants in the drama, it would be with the disciples, but the author works against such identification. We are privy to truths the disciples seem unable to grasp. Their almost incomprehensible blindness forces questions from us: How can they be so dull? How can they fail to see what is obvious? How can they fail to hear what even demons are forced to shout? Will they ever see clearly?

The relationship between disciples and demons takes one more interesting turn. While the disciples actually do begin to carry out their commission as exorcists ("They cast out many demons" [6:13]), there remains some question about their own immunity to unclean spirits. In the great transitional scene, when Peter confesses Jesus to be the Christ and Jesus predicts his impending death and resurrection, Jesus concludes what began as a promising moment with a rebuke of Peter, which follows Peter's rebuke of Jesus: "But turning and looking at his disciples, he rebuked Peter and said, 'Get behind me, Satan! For you are setting your mind not on divine things but on human things' " (8:33).

Why is Jesus' rebuke of Peter addressed to Satan? The particular verb, *epitimao,* appears infrequently in Mark, but the pattern of occurrences is significant. Jesus rebukes unclean spirits (1:25, 3:12, 9:25), and he rebukes the wind and the sea (4:39). In the only other occurrences of the verb outside this passage, the connotation is negative: the disciples rebuked people who brought children to Jesus (10:13), and people rebuked blind Bartimaeus as he cried out to Jesus (10:48).

How then are we to hear the first of the occurrences here in 8:30? Following Peter's confession, Jesus "*epetimesen* them that they speak about him to no one." This is rather different from Matthew's affirmation: "Blessed are you, Simon son of Jonah! For flesh and blood has not revealed this to you, but my Father in heaven" (Matt. 16:17). The cryptic comment in Mark is usually translated, "and he sternly ordered them not to tell . . ." Yet this would constitute the only nonpejorative use of *epitimao* in the Gospel, particularly striking in light of the two occurrences that follow immediately (Peter's rebuke of Jesus and Jesus' rebuke of Peter). How is the negative sense to be understood?

Perhaps we are to understand Peter's confession as we have understood the "confessions" of the demons. Perhaps Mark, like Matthew, attributes Peter's insight to inspiration. But inspiration by whom? If Peter and the disciples are addressed as Jesus addresses others who are possessed, perhaps we are to wonder if Peter's insight is not of the same order. Perhaps the narrator implies that Peter's confession is of supernatural origin, but akin to the confessions of the demoniacs. There are difficulties with such a view. Demons, in Mark at least, never call Jesus "Christ"; they use "Holy One of God," "Son of God," and "Son of the Most High God." But there is something compelling about the notion that Peter is rebuked as Satan. It is not just that his opposition to Jesus' suffering represents a replay of the temptation that precedes his public ministry (particularly because in Mark Jesus' testing is without content). It is perhaps rather that Peter's imagination is not his own. His inability to hold together his hopes and Jesus' predictions betrays an orientation that will lead in the wrong direction. His confession is not wrong; Jesus is the Christ, as we know from 1:1 and 14:61-62. But there is more to confession than getting the words right. That is one of the realities the story explores. Demons always speak the truth, although it means their undoing. Jesus' enemies speak the truth, identifying him as "the Messiah, the Son of the Blessed One" (14:61), "the King of the Jews" (15:2, 9, 12, 18, 26), "the Christ, the King of Israel" (15:32), and "God's Son" (15:39), although they have no idea that their words are true.[7]

---

7. See Juel, *Messiah and Temple* for commentary on these passages. I have come to believe that even "Son of God" in 15:39 ought probably be read as a taunt ("Sure, this was God's Son"), in accord with the rest of the taunts in the account of Jesus' trial and death. The centurion plays a role assigned all Jesus' enemies: They speak the truth in mockery, thus providing for the reader ironic testimony to the truth.

The right words are important, but they do not necessarily lead to life. Peter, like the rest of the disciples, has his mind set on human ways, not on God's.

If that is true, Peter, and the rest, will have to be set free. Satan will have to be exorcised from their imaginations. Only then will they be able to play their appointed role in the household assigned them by the lord of the house (13:33-37). They will not be able to free themselves any more than the demoniac, but Jesus has the power to cast out legions; he intends to bind the strong man and plunder his house. When? And how? At what point will the right words lead to life?

The dynamic that drives the story to its unsatisfying conclusion with frightened women at an empty tomb derives its energy from scenes like this one. Form critical studies of the pericope, while enlightening, miss precisely this aspect of engagement with the narrative. The dramatic exorcisms are part of a larger enterprise that is full of twists, turns, and surprises. The story of Jesus and the demoniac in the region of the Gerasenes creates expectations that will be met—or disappointed—in what follows. And such matters will prove in the long run to be the most significant for interpreters.

6

Watching and Weariness:
The So-Called Markan Apocalypse

Chapter 13 of Mark's Gospel stands out for several reasons, and it is not surprising that the "little apocalypse" has generated a considerable body of opinion among commentators. It is one of the few extended discourses by Jesus in Mark's Gospel. Further, it seems to break into the narrative with remarkably little attention to what precedes and what follows. No reference is made, for example, to Jesus' own impending death. The discourse is concerned exclusively with events that will occur beyond the conclusion of the narrative. Finally, the language of the discourse is unusual, particularly the imagery common to such works as Daniel and John's Apocalypse.

Study of the chapter has led in various directions. Since the middle of the nineteenth century, a body of scholarship has developed regarding the provenance of the material.[1] Historians are interested in the nature of Mark's sources, the circumstances that led to the rise of such a discourse, and perhaps in the possibility of tracing the material to Jesus himself.[2] Not surprisingly, more recent scholarship has demonstrated

---

1. Vincent Taylor, in *The Gospel according to St. Mark* (London: Macmillan, 1963; 1st ed. 1952), 498–99, traces the notion of a pre-Markan apocalypse to the nineteenth-century scholars T. Colani (*Jésus-Christ et les croyances messianiques de son temps* [Strasbourg, 1864]) and W. Weiffenbach (*Der Wiederkunftsgedanke Jesu* [1873]).

2. Taylor, *Mark*, provides a useful catalog of names and opinions up to the 1950s. Lars Hartman, in *Prophecy Interpreted: The Formation of Some Jewish Apocalyptic Tests and of the Eschatological Discourse Mark 13 par.*, trans. Neil Tomkinson, Coniectanea Biblica 1 (Lund: Gleerup, 1966), provides a useful overview of the scholarly discussion of the chapter as well.

less interest in pre-Markan tradition than in the function of the traditions in their present setting.[3]

A fascinating aspect of current scholarship has been the dominance of history-of-religions categories in the interpretation of the Bible. The designation "little apocalypse" is a case in point. While scholarship has shifted dramatically from interest in the history of the Gospel tradition to study of the narratives themselves, categories like "apocalyptic" persist in commentaries. While earlier generations of interpreters sought to distance the New Testament from "apocalyptic," since Käsemann's famous essay in the post–World War II period the category has enjoyed a favored position in New Testament circles.[4] And while defining precisely what is meant by "apocalyptic" has become more and more complex,[5] students of Mark have made wider and wider use of the category. In his New Testament Introduction, Norman Perrin entitles the section on Mark's Gospel, "The Apocalyptic Drama";[6] Howard Kee predicates his interpretation of Mark on a social analysis of "apocalyptic" communities, especially as identified by Daniel, the work which Kee argues provides the model for Mark's narrative, both in literary and ideological terms.[7]

One result of such an approach is that the Gospel narrative has been read from a particular literary or ideological perspective that is itself largely a scholarly artifice. Kee's analysis of Daniel, "the classic document produced in the apocalyptic category,"[8] provides a set of categories, he argues, that explain Mark's literary strategy, its underlying theological presuppositions, and its "life structure." Comments like these are typical:

3. This is most clearly the case in Jan Lambrecht, *Die Redaktion der Markus-Apokalypse*, AB 28 (Rome, 1967). Hartman (*Prophecy Interpreted*) is an exception, although his interest in the midrashic character of apocalyptic traditions and their development certainly does not preclude an interest in the final form of chapter 13. See the helpful discussion in Howard Kee, *Community of the New Age: Studies in Mark's Gospel* (Philadelphia: Westminster Press, 1977), 43–48, 64–74, who, however, is less interested in the function of chapter 13 in its present setting than in questions about its genre.

4. E. Käsemann, esp. "The Beginnings of Christian Theology" and "On the Subject of Primitive Christian Apocalyptic," in *New Testament Questions of Today* (Philadelphia: Fortress Press, 1969), 82–107 and 108–137, respectively.

5. Paul Hanson, *The Dawn of Apocalyptic: The Historical and Sociological Roots of Jewish Apocalyptic Eschatology* (Philadelphia: Fortress Press, 1979).

6. Norman Perrin, *The New Testament: An Introduction* (New York: Harcourt, Brace, Jovanovich, 1974).

7. Kee, *Community*, 64–74. The scholarly convention is the more striking in view of scholarship like Hartman's, whose use of terms like "midrashic" to characterize formal aspects of the traditions in Mark 13 ought to raise serious questions about the adequacy of older categories.

8. Kee, *Community*, 65.

The practical aim of the apocalyptists is not to make the insiders proud because they know what others do not, but to strengthen them to persevere in the face of the mounting hostility and suffering that confronts them.[9]

What has always struck me about Kee's analysis is how inadequate his categories seem to Mark's narrative. While Mark's Gospel makes repeated use of Daniel, most readers will be more impressed by the differences between Daniel and Mark than by their similarities. That is particularly true with regard to the visionary material in chapter 13. The so-called little apocalypse does not end the Gospel narrative; Jesus' forecast of what lies ahead introduces the passion story, the longest piece of coherent narrative in the Gospel. Étienne Trocmé's famous argument that Mark's "original" Gospel really ends with chapter 13 only highlights the differences between the present Gospel narrative and its alleged apocalyptic antecedents.[10] More interesting and promising are interpretations of the chapter whose primary focus is the function of the discourse within the Gospel narrative. Historical questions and investigations of the history of tradition are not without significance, but they are secondary to a reading of the narrative.

One of the most interesting among Markan commentators is the British scholar R. H. Lightfoot. His essays in *The Gospel Message of St. Mark*, published in 1950, are still among the most creative and interesting studies of the Gospel.[11] His comments on chapter 13 reflect an interest in literary strategy and a sense of the narrative whole:

> It will be remembered that, though St. Mark's Gospel concerns itself chiefly with the Lord's actions, there are two chapters, four and thirteen, which are remarkable for the exceptional amount of teaching or discourse which they contain. When we considered the earlier of these two chapters, that is, Mark 4:1-34, I suggested that the parables and sayings are recorded at this point, not so much in order to provide examples of the Lord's method of teaching and its content, as to give an assurance, in traditional sayings of the Lord which the evangelist found at his disposal, of the final, ultimate, certain success of His mission in spite of present, temporary difficulty and hindrance. . . . Probably the purpose of chapter 13 is largely similar, but now the horizon is far wider, and the surrounding darkness also very much greater. Chapter 13 is a great divine prophecy of the

---

9. *Ibid*, 74.

10. Trocmé, *The Formation of the Gospel according to Mark,* trans. P. Gaughan (Philadelphia: Westminster Press, 1975), esp. chap. 4, "The Two Editions of the Gospel according to Mark."

11. R. H. Lightfoot, *The Gospel Message of St. Mark* (Oxford: Clarendon Press, 1950).

ultimate salvation of the elect after and indeed through unprecedented and unspeakable suffering, trouble, and disaster.[12]

Lightfoot contends that the chapter has an important function as a preface to the passion story, even if Jesus' own death is not mentioned in the discourse:

> It would perhaps be generally agreed that chapter 13 is undoubtedly designed by the evangelist as the immediate introduction to the Passion narrative, in the sense that as we read the story of the Passion in this gospel in its utter realism and unrelieved tragedy we are to remember always the person and office of Him of whom we read. He, who is now reviled, rejected, and condemned is none the less the supernatural Son of man; and the terrible story of the last twenty-four hours has for its other side that eternal weight of glory which was reached and could only be reached, as the Church believed, through the Lord's death upon the cross, and through the sufferings of His disciples also.[13]

Lightfoot's specific suggestions about relationships between Jesus' discourse and the ensuing narrative are an invitation to a different sort of study, which I am convinced holds greater promise than those whose point of departure is a set of categories ("apocalyptic") or a history of tradition.

The Temple

Jesus' predictions of what lies ahead take as their point of departure the impending destruction of Jerusalem and the Temple. The discourse begins with an artificial comment on the Temple by the disciples: "Look, Teacher, what large stones and what large buildings!" (13:1). While the transition to the discourse from the preceding narrative is abrupt, there has been ample preparation for Jesus' warning about the Temple, and there is a logic in moving from the story of the widow's penny to the prediction of destruction.

The Temple is the center of attention from the moment Jesus arrives in Jerusalem. His triumphant procession leads immediately to the Temple (11:11). After cursing a fig tree on his way to the city, his first act upon arriving in the Temple on the following morning is to drive out sellers and money changers (11:15-17), thus spurring the Temple authorities to plot a way to kill him (11:18). We have known that the

12. Lightfoot, *Gospel Message*, 48.
13. *Ibid*, 50–51.

scribes, chief priests, and elders will "reject" Jesus since his first prediction of his rejection and vindication (8:31-33). It is implied, in fact,
early in the story when scribes claim that Jesus is guilty of blasphemy
(2:6-7). The moment at which plans against Jesus begin to crystalize
likewise signals the beginning of the end for Jerusalem: Jesus' "cursing"
of the Temple, drawing on scriptural material from Isaiah 56 and Jer-
emiah 7, marks the Temple for destruction.

The ensuing discussion takes up the issue, first with Jesus' parable
about the wicked tenants whose foolish action against the owner's son
will bring their demise (12:1-11). The leaders of the Temple establishment—the scribes, chief priests, and elders—plot how to destroy Jesus,
because they know that he has told the parable against them (12:12).
Jesus' citation of Psalm 118:22 (12:11), and the employment in the
parable itself of imagery from Isaiah 5:1-2 (12:1)—imagery that in the
Isaiah Targum is applied detail for detail to the destruction of the
Temple[14]—provide scriptural warrant for the events to follow. The biblical material likewise serves to interpret the Temple's coming demise.[15]

The Temple appears again in an unlikely place, in the discussion
between Jesus and a scribe about the commandment that should be
viewed as "first of all" (12:28-34). In response to Jesus' traditional
summary of the law in terms of the commands to love God and the
neighbor, the scribe says:

> You are right, Teacher; you have truly said that "he is one, and besides
> him there is no other"; and "to love him with all the heart, and with all
> the understanding, and with all the strength," and "to love one's neighbor
> as oneself"—this is much more important than all whole burnt offerings
> and sacrifices." (12:32-33)

The contrast between keeping the commandments and "all whole
burnt offerings and sacrifices"—a contrast not implied either in Deuteronomy or in Leviticus—prepares the audience at least indirectly for
the impending destruction of the Temple and Jesus' prediction.

The story of the widow who contributes all she had to live on to
the Temple that immediately precedes Jesus' discourse provides an interesting transition from controversies with the Temple authorities to

14. See Juel, *Messiah and Temple*, SBLDS 31 (Missoula, Mont.: Scholars Press, 1977),
136–37.

15. Some commentators speak here of the "rejection of Israel." There is no justification
for such a reading. The polemic is directed at the Temple and its leaders. The use of
biblical material among Jewish interpreters to understand the Temple's destruction (as,
e.g., in the Isaiah Targum noted above) indicates that the Scriptures could function as
self-critical or as weapons for debate within the Jewish community. See Juel, *Messiah and
Temple*, and Trocmé, *The Formation*, 206–8.

the actual forecast of its destruction. After having beaten the religious authorities at their own game of scriptural interpretation (12:35-37), Jesus issues a series of warnings against the religious:

> Beware of the scribes, who like to walk around in long robes, and to be greeted with respect in the market places, and to have the best seats in the synagogues and places of honor at banquets! *They devour widows' houses* and for the sake of appearance say long prayers. They will receive the greater condemnation. (Mark 12:38-40)

The story of the widow who contributes her last coins—"all she had to live on"—serves not simply to emphasize true generosity—"an example of total self-giving on the eve of the passion"; it is a graphic example of Jesus' charge that the religious leaders live off the poor and the helpless rather than caring for them. A poor widow gives her last penny to an institution that has become a "bandit's den." The move to Jesus' prediction that the Temple will be destroyed is thus motivated by the story that precedes it. The promised condemnation of the scribes takes shape in the prediction that not one stone will be left on another in Jerusalem.

The theme is picked up again at Jesus' trial, where witnesses testify falsely against Jesus about an alleged threat against "this temple that is made with hands" and a promise that "in three days I will build another, not made with hands" (14:58). The restatement of the charge in the mockery at the foot of the cross (15:29) and the terse reference to the ripping of the Temple curtain at the moment of Jesus' death (15:38) mark with finality the certainty of the Temple's end—leaving open the possibility that Jesus will provide something in its place, "another [temple], not made with hands."[16]

While links between Jesus' prediction of Jerusalem's destruction in chapter 13 and preceding and subsequent chapters may not be explicit, the thematic ties at least are obvious. Preparation for the future involves having some sense about why the Temple must be destroyed and what impact that absence will have.

Beyond the Ending

Lightfoot's observations about the connections between chapter thirteen and the ensuing narrative are focused christologically. He argues that the despised and rejected Jesus must also be the one who will return

16. On this see Juel, *Mark,* Augsburg Commentary Series (Minneapolis: Augsburg Books, 1990), and *Messiah and Temple,* 143–57.

with the clouds of heaven, in order to understand the passion story. Jesus' predictions point beyond the story as it ends in chapter 16; they anticipate a genuine future beyond the women's silence. A suggestion that the chapter should be viewed as a farewell discourse or last testament was made as early as 1938 by F. Busch.[17] The suggestion is taken up briefly by Nils Dahl in his 1958 article, "The Purpose of Mark's Gospel."[18] While it would prove difficult to establish that the chapter is formally similar to farewell discourses, it is significant that like such last testaments, Jesus' discourse points beyond the confines of the story. It is not simply an introduction to the passion story.

Jesus' extended discourse is not the only prophetic piece in the Gospel, although it is the longest. On numerous occasions promises are made that point beyond the ending of Mark's story. Sometimes those earlier forecasts provide a context for hearing chapter thirteen. Warnings of family conflicts (13:12-13), for example, are anticipated both by earlier statements about family disruption (3:31-35; 10:29) as well as by the promise of a new family in 10:30. Jesus' comment about leaving families and houses and fields "for my sake and for the sake of the good news" surely point to the era when "the good news" is the message preached to all the nations (13:10), as Marxsen argued some time ago.[19] The promise that the good news will be preached to all the nations, while stated in the passive, must presume that the disciples will be the first preachers; while the "you" in Jesus' predictions is not limited to the disciples (13:37), it surely does address them. Here, earlier promises are critical as well. James and John are among the inner circle to whom Jesus speaks, after all, and he has promised earlier that they will drink the cup and be baptized with the baptism he is undergoing (10:38-40). The injunction to Peter, James, and John to tell no one about the events of the mount of Transfiguration "until the Son of Man rise from the dead" (9:9) presume such a future as well. And the instructions about waiting for the Holy Spirit to give the words for testimony (13:11) probably take up John the baptizer's promise that Jesus "will baptize you with the Holy Spirit" (1:8), the first of the many promises that await fulfillment beyond the confines of the story Mark tells.

17. F. Busch, *Zum Verständnis der synoptischen Eschatologie: Markus 13 neu untersucht* (Gütersloh: Bertelsmann, 1938).

18. Nils Alstrup Dahl, "The Purpose of Mark's Gospel," *Jesus in the Memory of the Early Church* (Minneapolis: Augsburg Books, 1976); first published as "Markusevangeliets sikte" in SEA 22/23 (1958): 62–63.

19. W. Marxsen, *Mark the Evangelist,* trans. J. Boyce, et. al. (Nashville: Abingdon, 1969).

Jesus' warnings point beyond the confines of the story, and they do so in the context of promises, as in chapter 4—as Lightfoot argued. The Parable of the Sower promises that there will be failure and disappointment—but a harvest that will make the enterprise worthwhile. Chapter 13 functions in a similar way. Terrible difficulties—the tribulations—await the disciples and their contemporaries. The events that will mark Jerusalem's destruction are only the beginning of the birth pangs (13:8). But they will mark the onset of birth pangs—a technical term within apocalyptic tradition that can identify signs of hope even at times of intense suffering. As in nature growth and harvest follow planting, so suffering and pain accompany the process of birth. Both processes drive toward a positive outcome: harvest and new birth. However dark the days, Jesus promises that "all will see" the return of the Son of Man coming in clouds with great power and glory (13:26).

"I Have Already Told You Everything"

One important difference between the prophetic material in Mark and in a work like Daniel is that it does not appear at the end of the work. While Jesus' prophetic words point to the future beyond the Gospel's end, they function as an introduction to the passion story. Lightfoot argues that they do so in order to provide a necessary setting within which to hear the account of Jesus' rejection "in its utter realism and unrelieved tragedy."

The passion story likewise provides dramatic confirmation that the picture Jesus sketches of the world in which discipleship will be lived out is accurate. The world will prove inhospitable. Jesus warns that they will "hand you over to councils" (13:9); he himself is handed over. He warns that his followers "will be beaten in synagogues"; he himself is beaten both by Jewish and Roman attendants. He promises that they will have to give testimony "before governors and kings"; Jesus must appear before Pilate where he is asked to testify on his own behalf.[20] And "brother will betray brother to death," he tells them; one of his brothers, Judas, betrays him with a kiss (14:10, 43-46). Given the use of family imagery to speak of Jesus' followers (3:31-35 and 10:30), the collapse of his circle anticipates the internal conflicts about which Jesus

20. Matthew speaks of Pilate as "governor" (*hegemon*) (Matt. 27:2, 11, 14, 15, 21, 27; 28:14), while Mark does not. My argument for intentional parallels would be stronger, obviously, if Mark employed the term.

warns the inner circle. Through the darkness at Jesus' crucifixion, nature itself testifies to the cosmic scope of the dark times ahead. While there is no one-to-one correspondence between Jesus' forecast and the ensuing narrative, there is enough to attract attention. The world for which he prepares his followers is precisely the world that has no room for him. If chapter 13 serves to introduce the account of Jesus' passion with ultimate promises, it also paints the future in somber colors. The world that finds Jesus an intolerable threat and disappointment will not soon change. It will provide genuine danger to the faithful. While the harvest lies ahead, what is of immediate concern are all the obstacles to growth.

Stay Awake

Jesus' discourse in Mark 13 concludes with a short parable about a householder and his slaves that merits more attention than it has received from commentators.[21] Kee's categorization of apocalyptic literature as intended to "strengthen people to persevere" in the face of hostility and persecution fits the little parable not at all. Were Jesus' discourse intended to exhort the faithful to persevere, we might have expected his warnings to conclude with verse 13 ("But the one who endures to the end will be saved") or verse 23 ("But be alert; I have already told you everything"). The danger to which Jesus' concluding image addresses itself, however, is not faltering in the face of persecution, but falling asleep.

The little parable, in fact, sets a tone quite different from what one might have expected from an "apocalyptic" discourse. The master in the parable—in its narrative setting, clearly a reference to Jesus—addresses his slaves as members of a household, an image we have encountered elsewhere in Mark (3:25-27; 10:28-30) and that is familiar within the New Testament from epistolary literature, where it is employed for moral exhortation.[22] The household imagery implies a kind of order and stability. The master of the house gives to his slaves "the

---

21. Remarkably, Hartmann (*Prophecy Interpreted*) makes only a single reference to the concluding verses in the chapter (p. 175), so that it is unclear whether he believes the verses were added later (after Matthew and Luke composed their Gospels) or simply that the verses are only loosely attached to the preceding material in terms of the history of tradition. Because he is not interested in Mark but in the prior history of the material, however, his lack of interest in the verses is perhaps understandable. Kee's single reference to these verses is less understandable, because he is interested in the interpretation of Mark (*Community of the New Age*, 161).

22. David Balch, *Let Wives Be Submissive: The Domestic Codes in I Peter* (Chico, Calif.: Scholars Press, 1981).

authority"; each receives a task to perform. The greatest danger is that the slave on watch will drop off and that the master will return to find his slaves asleep. The RSV translation, "Watch!" did not quite capture the contrast between sleep and wakefulness. Jesus enjoins his faithful to stay awake, and he extends the injunction to others: "What I say to you I say to all: Keep awake" (Mark 13:37, NRSV).

On this note the narrative resumes. Events move quickly to their ordained conclusion. It is not long before the same faithful inner circle, asked to pray with Jesus before his ordeal, cannot stay awake. Twice Jesus asks the disciples to keep awake (14:34, 38); three times we are told he returns to find them sleeping (14:37, 40, 41). They are unable to reply to Jesus (14:40), and they appear utterly unprepared for his arrest. They all flee, with the exception of Peter who remains long enough to deny Jesus three times.

The disciples' problem is not that they are discouraged or unable to endure in the face of pressure but that they are utterly unprepared. Believing Jesus to be the Christ and anticipating the coming of the Kingdom, they are concerned with position—even with places of honor at Jesus' right and left (10:37). They have no idea what will be involved in taking places at the right and left of the "King of the Jews" (15:27). Peter and the rest can promise to remain steadfast no matter what the cost (14:29, 31), but without any sense of the dangers the future holds. As Jesus prays for his life, they sleep. And when the crisis comes, they run.

"Keep awake" is quite different from "Hold fast." The sense of being surprised and caught off guard is amplified in Matthew's version of Jesus' discourse, where wakefulness is developed in several stories about servants and households, and about the ten maidens who were to light the bridegroom's way to the wedding banquet (Matt. 24:45—25:46). While Matthew's stories stress accountability in view of impending judgment, the parable in Mark focuses more on insensitivity to the situation.

Insensitivity relates most immediately to the disciples. They are the ones caught off guard; they are the ones who cannot remain awake. The passive construction, "their eyes were weighed down" (14:40, author's translation), is reminiscent of the images of blindness, deafness, and hardness of heart employed earlier (6:52; 8:17). Such language reveals the inadequacy of interpretations that see the disciples as foils for the ideal reader. They do not perform as they must if they are to carry out their commissions as Jesus' fellow preachers and healers (3:14-15), but their problems are not of the sort that will be solved by greater resolve. Eyes and ears must be opened; hardened hearts must be softened. If the disciples cannot stay awake, something will have to be done to rouse them from their slumber—something akin, perhaps, to action necessary to raise Jesus from the dead.

And the story does promise such a dramatic rehabilitation. If the good news must be preached to all the nations (13:10), the role of the disciples must be presumed. The parable about the householder and the household offers some glimpse of what readers should expect. Jesus, the "stronger one" whose goal was to despoil Satan's household and who promises to the faithful a new household in this age (10:29-30), speaks of himself as "master of the house." Jesus' inner circle of disciples are invited to imagine the future in terms of a household in which they will be given authority and tasks to perform (13:34). The use of institutional imagery is unmistakable. And while the "you" being addressed is expanded to include readers (13:37), Jesus is speaking to followers who have been instructed about the exercise of authority (10:42-43); they have been told already that those who are to lead must be slaves of all (10:44). While Jesus promises that they will all flee, even Peter, he promises to precede them to Galilee (14:28-30).

The disciples are not simply foils for readers whose privileged position allows for a certain disdain. It never ceases to amaze me that commentators take a kind of delight in the disciples' failures. There are few readings of the Gospel that elicit any empathy with those whose eyes were very heavy, and fewer still who pick up on the promises of their rehabilitation. While readers cannot identify with the disciples—we are located at a different plane from the beginning of the story—something about their plight is instructive. Nowhere is that clearer than in the case of Jesus' eschatological discourse. Within its narrative setting, at least, the discourse functions almost exclusively for the benefit of readers who live beyond the time of the story; the discourse forms a bridge between story time and the situation of an audience. And if that is not clear enough, readers are directly addressed in the concluding verse: "What I say to you I say to all: Keep awake" (13:37).

The disciples can do nothing about the warning. As the forces of darkness gather, their eyes are weighed down (14:40). What of the next generation of believers?

Sleepy Believers

In 1958, Nils Dahl published a short article in Norwegian titled "Markusevangeliets sikte," translated as "The Purpose of Mark's Gospel."[23]

---

23. *Jesus in the Memory of the Early Church* (Minneapolis: Augsburg Books, 1976), 52–65. The original essay appeared in SEA 22/23 (1958).

In it, he argued that rather than presuming a readership whose problem was persecution, he argued that the Gospel addresses a church that has tasted success and found it satisfying. It envisions believers who have taken the gospel for granted, who no longer see the world painted in dramatic colors. The story of Jesus is retold to shock them into awareness.

I have always been struck by Dahl's characterization of Mark's implied readership; it seems more apt now than it did when I first read the essay. The little parable of the master of the house that concludes Jesus' predictions of what awaits the faithful casts the warnings in a particular light. The risk is not that they will lose heart in the face of persecution but that they will drift off, oblivious to the dangers and the possibilities that lie ahead.

The chapter anticipates the final end of things; the eschatological sequence initiated by the destruction of Jerusalem seems likewise apparent. Kelber is surely correct in stressing that "the end is still to come" (13:7).[24] The period prior to the return of Jesus in the clouds is the critical time. The little parable speaks of a household in which slaves have authority; we might even imagine they have the luxury of time for bickering about position and debating who is the greatest. Part of their enterprise is to preach the good news. Evidence for such a construct is provided by epistolary literature that employs precisely such imagery in its portrayals of the church.

The disciples do not heed Jesus' warning. They are perhaps among the sinners Jesus came to call (2:17); his life will apparently be given as a ransom for them as well (10:45). If there is a promise here, however, it must be related to the corresponding threat. The setting presumed by the narrative—the implied setting of the implied reader—suggests a settled community with familiar institutional concerns.[25] Here the traditional "apocalyptic" reading of the chapter fails. For the disciples in the story, the reality of Jesus' forecasts comes as a terrible surprise. The same may well be true for later generations of Mark's readers, whose confidence may be as misplaced as that of the disciples, whose eyes may be as blind to the obstacles and threats to the gospel as those of the disciples. There is promise, but one must know where to look and what to listen for.

Jesus' discourse, which concludes with the little parable, addresses a readership whose greatest danger is not a failure of nerve as much as a tired lack of awareness both of the dangers and the possibilities that lie ahead.

24. W. Kelber, *The Kingdom in Mark* (Philadelphia: Fortress Press, 1974).
25. See "The Markan Community," chap. 9, below.

Part Three

THE FUTURE
OF A SURPRISE

7

The Death of the King:
The Origin of Mark's Christology

The designation "the death of the King" in the chapter title should be read in two different senses. It is first a literary assessment of Mark's narrative. The story of Jesus climaxes in his trial and death as king. "Christ, the King of Israel" and "King of the Jews" are the terms employed by major characters in the story. The amount of space devoted to the account, the prominent location of the trial and crucifixion scenes at the climax of the story, and the recurrence of royal imagery suggest the aptness of such an assessment.

"The death of the King" is also construed in an historical sense, as is clear in the second part of the chapter title, "the Origin of Mark's Christology." In reading the Gospel, it is not necessary to ask questions about origin, as has become more apparent in recent scholarship. Questions of origin are quite legitimate, however, and may even prove to be crucial in the literary enterprise. One purpose of this chapter is to explore the relationship between literary assessment and historical reconstruction as aspects of biblical interpretation. While I am principally interested in engagement with the narrative, I continue to regard as important historical questions about the world outside and behind the narrative. How the various approaches to Mark's Christology are finally related is the point at issue.

Before proceeding some clarifications are in order: One is to establish what is meant by Mark in the expression Mark's Christology. That may seem rather obvious. In view of the last decades of scholarship, however, more clarity is in order. By Mark I refer to the implied author of the book known as the Gospel according to Mark. The implied author is the personality—the sum total of the perspectives and judgments, the rhetorical strategies, the promises and disappointments—that emerges from the overall work. We may or may not be able to establish a link between the anonymous narrator and an identifiable, flesh-and-blood person from the early Christian movement. We can presume the work was written by one individual and not a group, and it is even possible that some of the traditions about the author, beginning with the testimony of Papias, are reliable. On the other hand, interpretation cannot await a scholarly consensus regarding so speculative a matter as identification of the author of the Gospel, who chose to remain anonymous. Even without a consensus regarding the flesh-and-blood author, however, we can still speak of the author in the sense of the "implied author," as the personality behind the overall perspective of the Gospel. By Mark then I mean that implied author. I am dubious about the historical reliability of the tradition that views the composer of this work as an intimate of Peter, but that will not be a major factor in interpreting the finished product.

As a matter of equal importance, I wish to distinguish this implied author from the Mark isolated by redaction critics. Particularly since the work of Willi Marxsen, scholars have identified Mark as the editor responsible for shaping and modifying traditional material, whose hand is clearest in summaries and seams. The perspective of this redactor has been derived by redaction critics, largely from the small group of summaries and the obvious modifications of tradition. Redaction critics have consequently seen their primary interpretive task as that of distinguishing tradition from redaction. Such an approach suggests that the author's perspective is known only to the degree he disagreed with and modified the tradition. What is Markan comes to be identified with a small portion of the work. Not only does such an approach presume an unrealistic ability to distinguish tradition from redaction; it also must discount most of the literary work as relevant for describing the perspective of the author. I believe such a procedure is highly misleading. Distinguishing Markan Christology from the views of earlier tradition expressed in the sources of his Gospel will not be the primary goal of this study. Markan Christology refers to the perspective of the work as a whole—presuming that such a perspective can be identified.

I wish to limit my work further by focusing on a critical theme in Mark's Christology: Messianism. Once again, arguments for the significance of Messianism and Messiah for Mark's assessment of Jesus will derive largely from close readings of the text. While it is not necessary to know Mark's sources to understand his work, it is helpful, perhaps even crucial, to understand the historical and traditional setting of the language he employs. Mark, like other Christians, sought to offer an assessment of Jesus and his ministry in terms of traditional imagery drawn from the Jewish Scriptures as they were understood in the first century. The fundamental category in Mark's view of Jesus is that of Messiah (Greek *Christos*), a conception that has roots in the Jewish Bible but that had a history in post-biblical Jewish circles prior to its use by Jesus' followers. We should be clear about the relationship between New Testament exegesis and historical reconstruction. Demonstration of the importance of the concept Messiah (Christ) in Mark requires exegetical argument. Historical studies regarding the previous history of Messiah cannot establish the significance of the term for Mark, although they have an important role to play in interpretation. What the title meant in the tradition available to Mark and his readers, and what the traditional meaning contributes to our understanding of Mark, are matters of considerable importance for our exegesis.

Attempts at historical reconstruction of post-biblical messianic tradition, of course, will view Mark's Gospel as a significant piece of evidence. In his story, a variety of characters offer their assessment of Jesus. Particularly in the passion sequence, religious and political leaders provide a sense of how the title "the Christ" sounds as an epithet for Jesus. Their views, which to a considerable extent clash with those of the narrator and his readers, may offer important clues to the meaning of Messiah in post-biblical Jewish tradition. Other post-biblical Jewish literature can confirm or disconfirm such clues as historically helpful. Proposed interpretations of Mark that are able to make sense of the evidence in light of what is known from other contemporary sources will assume greater plausibility. My primary task is to examine Mark, although I am most interested in the results of studies of extra- and pre-Markan tradition.

"The Christ" in Mark

A brief survey of the concordance indicates that the title "the Christ," although used relatively infrequently, may well qualify as the preeminent title in the Gospel. It occurs with about the same frequency as "the Son of God" (or related terms like "Son of the Most High" or "My Son"), a title whose significance has long been recognized, and it appears in crucial situations. Particularly significant are two passages: the confession of Peter in 8:29 and the question of the high priest in 14:61. The latter passage provides something of a climax in the story. The chief priest asks the decisive question, using titles that appear together only in the opening sentence of Mark's Gospel (if we are to adopt the reading of Nestles' 26th edition): "Are you the Christ, the Son of the Blessed?" Jesus—for the first and only time in the story—gives an unambiguous statement about his identity: "I am" (14:62). The exchange between Jesus and the high priest surely provides one of the story's climaxes, ensuring Jesus' death and forcing the Jewish court to make a decision about the alleged Christ. The place of the title "the Christ" in such a passage is reason enough to pay particular attention to the epithet.

The expression "the Son of Man" is of course the most frequent epithet in the Gospel. It ought not, however, be considered a title in the same way as "Christ" and "Son of God." It never appears as a predicate in a statement like, "You are the Son of Man." It occurs exclusively on the lips of Jesus. And whatever one may think of pre-Markan tradition, in Mark "the Son of Man" is always to be understood as Jesus' self-designation. Its absence in any assessment of Jesus and its exclusive use as a self-reference by Jesus ought to caution against speaking of a "Son of Man" Christology. There is little exegetical warrant for such an alleged Son of Man Christology, which must rely almost exclusively on (often fanciful) historical speculation.[1] In 14:62, Jesus' promise that his judges " 'will see the Son of Man seated at the right hand of the Power,' and 'coming with the clouds of heaven' " does not represent a qualification of the messianic epithets but a promise that the claim will be vindicated. It is similar in function to 13:26, where the return of the Son of Man will be the occasion for vindicating those who have ignored the "false Christs and false prophets" (13:22) and remained faithful to the true Christ. On that occasion, all "will see."

Exegetical data suggest the importance of the concept "Messiah" for understanding Mark's Christology. The data also exhibit patterns that require interpretation:

1. "Christ" appears in 1:1, then (apart from the variant reading in 1:34) not again until Peter's confession in 8:29. Virtually the whole of Jesus' public ministry passes without the suggestion that he is the Messiah. Herod fears that he is John the Baptist raised from the dead (6:14; 8:27-28); the common people regard him as a prophet, perhaps Elijah. It is not until Peter's confession, which is probably to be understood not so much as an assessment of what Jesus has done as an anticipation of what he is yet to do, that anyone uses the title "the Christ."

2. The greatest concentration of uses of the term "Christ" is in the last section of Mark, in particular the passion story, where Jesus

---

1. Regarding the use of the term in the New Testament and associations with Daniel 7, see Juel, *Messianic Exegesis* (Minneapolis: Fortress Press, 1990), 151–70.

is interrogated as "the Christ, the Son of the Blessed," and is mocked as "the Christ, the King of Israel." The latter phrase, used by the chief priests and the scribes in 15:32, identifies "the Christ" as a royal figure. Related to Jewish use of the term "the Christ" is the Roman "the King of the Jews." It seems obvious from the passion account that "the Christ" is understood as a royal epithet, whatever scriptural possibilities may have existed for speaking about "anointing."[2] If "the Christ" and "the King" are to be understood as synonymous, it becomes clear that the passion narrative is dominated by "messianic"—that is, royal—imagery. The word "Christ" is used twice, "King of the Jews" five times. Jesus is tried, mocked, and executed as "the Christ, the Son of the Blessed One," "the Christ, the King of Israel," and "the King of the Jews."

3. Though there is some ambiguity about Jesus' attitude toward the title "Christ" in 8:30, there can be no doubt that according to Mark, Jesus regards the title as an appropriate designation. When the high priest asks Jesus the decisive question, "Are you the Christ, the Son of the Blessed One," he replies with an unambiguous answer: "I am; and 'you will see . . .' " The promise that his judges will see him enthroned and returning with the clouds in no sense modifies his claim to be the Christ but rather promises that there will be a spectacular vindication of that claim. The promise is couched in scriptural language, specifically drawn from Daniel 7 and Psalm 110. From the vantage point of the narrator, the confession that "Jesus is the Christ" is true.

4. The Gospel provides ample evidence that calling Jesus "the Christ" involves some difficulty. Characters in the story tell us how the confession sounds. After Peter confesses Jesus as "the Christ," he responds to Jesus' forecast of rejection, death, and resurrection by rebuking him. Peter is in turn rebuked, because his mind is focused on human rather than divine ways (8:31-33). Peter finds the combination of Messiahship and suffering incongruous.

The chief priest offers the next estimate. "Are you the Christ, the Son of the Blessed One?" he asks. At Jesus' response, he tears his robes—suggesting that the claim is blasphemous.[3] The mockery of the guards,

2. On the use of "the Christ" as a royal epithet in Mark, see Juel, *Messiah and Temple: The Trial of Jesus in the Gospel of Mark,* SBLDS 31 (Missoula, Mont.: Scholars Press, 1977), and Frank Matera, *The Kingship of Jesus,* SBLDS 66 (Chico, Calif.: Scholars Press, 1982).

3. The relationship between the charge of blasphemy and Jesus' statement has been a matter of considerable scholarly debate. For a discussion of various options, see Juel, *Messiah and Temple,* 95–106. In a paper presented at the annual meeting of the SBL in

including the taunt that Jesus should "prophesy," suggests that the messianic claim and the attendant promise of vindication strike the court as outrageous.

The Roman soldiers offer an estimate of how the confession sounds to non-Jews. They understand that Christ means "King." As befits their status as non-Israelites, they speak of this kingship exclusively in political terms. They call him "the King of the Jews," appropriately employing the term "Jew" to refer to Israelites. They dress Jesus in royal garb and pay him mock homage. It is as "King of the Jews" that Pilate executes Jesus. The soldiers' behavior and Pilate's formulation of the charge indicate that the claim Jesus is the King is—from the Roman perspective—both seditious and comical.

The mockery of Jesus as he hangs on the cross plays on his name (Jeshua = Savior: "He saved others; he cannot save himself" [15:31]), but the claim to be "the Messiah, the King of Israel" also appears in the taunt (15:31-32). Jesus' inability to save himself and to descend from the cross is taken as evidence that he is not the promised king and deliverer.

Even if we had no access to post-biblical Jewish literature, like the Psalms of Solomon 17 and 18, we could hazard a guess as to the meaning of "the Messiah." It is a royal term, we would infer from Mark, and its associations in post-biblical Jewish tradition suggest that to claim Jesus as Messiah is absurd. Mark does nothing to minimize the problem; he plays on it.

Various attempts have been made to derive the term "Messiah" from nonroyal traditions in post-biblical Judaism and thus avoid the problem posed by the nonmessianic character of the career of Jesus the Messiah.[4] When such alleged nonroyal messianic tradition is used to interpret Mark, however, the passion narrative makes no sense, for Mark's story is predicated on the tension between what everyone thinks and expects of the Messiah and what is in fact the case. Mark's story is deeply ironic, and the irony is bound up with the royal imagery that dominates Mark's

---

1989, Robert Gundry offered the intriguing suggestion that the circumlocutions for God's name reported in Jesus' reply to the chief priest would have been demanded in any recounting of the story, because to use the name in the recounting would itself constitute blasphemy. While this may be true, it does not settle the matter.

4. Prominent among those who have attempted such a derivation from the prophetic tradition are Klaus Burger, "Zum Problem der Messianität Jesu," *ZTK* 71 (1974): 1–30, and "Die königlichen Messiastraditionen des Neuen Testaments," NTS 20 (1973–74): 1–44; and A. E. Harvey, *Jesus and the Constraints of History* (London: Duckworth, 1982). Burger's work is particularly notable for its impact on the massive project of Edward Schillebeeckx.

narrative of the passion. As readers, we know that Jesus is the Christ (1:1; 14:62, inter alia). The great irony is that it is Jesus' enemies who invest him as king and pay homage. They offer testimony to what the reader knows to be the truth. Of course Jesus' enemies, whether Jewish or Roman, do not understand in what sense the words they speak are true. Jewish leaders regard the claim to be blasphemous and absurd; Romans view the claim as seditious and outrageous. Nevertheless, they speak the truth—contrary to their intentions and beyond their ability to understand. The irony in the story is pronounced, but it only works if Jesus is the Christ—and if the religious and political leaders speak for the tradition and common sense. Even if it were possible to demonstrate that the title "Messiah" could be used in the first century to refer to a prophetic and not a royal figure, such a derivation could not explain the way Mark's passion narrative employs messianic tradition.

The Messiah as David's Son

The claim that the traditional title "the Messiah" is central to Mark's Christology must deal with a problematic passage, where Jesus seems to take issue with traditional messianic categories:

> And as Jesus taught in the temple, he said, "How can the scribes say that the Messiah is the son of David? David himself, by the Holy Spirit, declared,
> 'The Lord said to my Lord,
> Sit at my right hand,
> until I put your enemies under your feet.'
> David himself calls him Lord; so how can he be his son?"
> (Mark 12: 35-37)

This controversy has been included in Mark within a section of controversies that precede Jesus' arrest, trial, and death. His opponents are religious officials—the scribes, chief priests, and elders. The issues that provide the focus of controversy were of considerable import to the Jewish community in the later decades of the first century—and presumably to Mark's audience.[5]

If we assume that these verses are consonant with the rest of Mark's Gospel—and we ought to make such an assumption until every effort to understand a particular passage within its narrative setting has failed— we should first observe that nowhere else in the Gospel is there a suggestion that Jesus is not the "Son of David." The confession of blind

---

5. See "The Markan Community," chap. 9 in this volume.

Bartimaeus in 10:47 suggests that the title is quite appropriate. The beggar who is blind is commended for his faith, and sees what Jesus' disciples (and his enemies) do not. The crowds acclaim Jesus as he rides into Jerusalem on a donkey with a line from Psalms, "Blessed is the one who comes in the name of the LORD!"(Ps. 118:26), followed by, "Blessed is the coming kingdom of our ancestor David!" (Mark 11:9-10). To argue that Jesus could accept the designation "the Christ, the Son of the Blessed One" from the high priest (14:61-62), while insisting that he is not "the Son of David" is improbable, whether we are considering the actual words of Jesus or Mark's story world. The little evidence that Jewish tradition knew of a non-Davidic Messiah is relatively late, and the notion of a Messiah ben Joseph would do little to clarify Jesus' comments in Mark 12. Attempts to prove that "the Messiah" could refer to a priestly or a prophetic figure are likewise unconvincing, and in any case such a derivation would also do little to clarify the problem Jesus poses for his opponents by quoting Psalm 110.

The comments are enigmatic, but it seems best to view the juxtaposition of "the Son of David" and "Lord" in Jesus' comments within the category of alleged scriptural contradictions familiar from rabbinic tradition.[6]

In this case, the view of the scribes that "the Christ is David's son" may be a shorthand substitution for the actual citation of passages such as 2 Sam. 7:12-14 or Ps. 89:3-4. This scriptural view is juxtaposed against another, the opening verse from Psalm 110, which seems to call into question what the Bible says elsewhere. (Jesus' question presumes his learned audience knows that Ps. 110:1 refers to the Messiah; he does not have to argue interpretation). Although the form of the pericope differs from that of the surrounding controversies, we must assume that Jesus' concluding question implies an answer to the problem he poses. A point has been made that made sense to the audience.

It seems most likely, as Evald Loevestam has argued, that the implied solution to the problem Jesus has posed—a possible contradiction within the Scriptures—is provided by events the readers know will soon follow. Jesus, the Son of David, rejected by the Temple authorities, will be raised from the dead and enthroned at God's right hand (cf. Jesus' promise in Mark 14:62, alluding to Ps. 110:1). It is appropriate for

6. Representative interpretations of this passage are discussed in Evald Loevestam's "Die Davidssohnsfrage," SEA 27 (1972): 72–82. In the essay he argues convincingly the case I am presenting. See also the comments by Wm. Lane, *The Gospel according to Mark*, NICNT (Grand Rapids: Eerdmans, 1974); and Nils A. Dahl, "Contradictions in Scripture," in *Studies in Paul* (Minneapolis: Augsburg Books, 1977), 159–77.

David to call his messianic son "Lord" in view of Jesus' installation at God's right hand. In fact, only if Jesus, the Son of David, has been elevated to that position does the alleged scriptural contradiction disappear. As in rabbinic tradition, the alleged contradiction is used to make a point—here, that death and resurrection are not incompatible with what the Scriptures have to say about the Christ. Because tradition knew nothing of a crucified Messiah, it could hardly have any conceptions of a resurrected king. The use of Psalm 110 to construct a scriptural image of a dying and rising Messiah is an example of creative Christian exegesis.[7]

The advantage of this interpretation is that it is compatible with what we know of post-biblical messianic tradition and does not result in contradictions within Mark. The passage presumes no distinction between an earthly and a heavenly deliverer. Rather, as in Acts, Ps. 110:1 becomes part of an argument according to which God's promise to David of a "seed" to sit on his throne forever (2 Sam. 7:12-14, Ps. 89:3-4) is fulfilled only with the installation of the risen Christ in heaven.[8] It is as the enthroned "Lord" that Jesus is Son of David.

"Son of God" as a Messianic Epithet

Related to Mark's use of "Messiah" is the use of the title "the Son of God." Although there may be other components in the title, royal overtones are unmistakable. The most obvious connection is in the question of the high priest (14:61), where "the Messiah" and "the Son of the Blessed One" are in apposition.[9] Two other occurrences are equally convincing. In both the baptismal story and the Transfiguration, God himself addresses Jesus as "Son"—using language from the messianic oracle in Psalm 2, where God calls the anointed king "my son" (see

---

7. David Hay, *Glory at the Right Hand: Psalm 110 in Early Christianity,* SBLMS 18 (Nashville: Abingdon, 1973). See also Juel, *Messianic Exegesis.*

8. This is precisely the argument in Peter's speech in Acts 2, where the reference to Psalm 132 (or 89), "he knew that God had sworn with an oath to him that he would put one of his descendants on his throne" (Acts 2:30), is enlisted with Ps. 110:1 in the proof that "God has made him both Lord and Messiah, this Jesus whom you crucified" (Acts 2:36). See Juel, "Social Dimensions of Exegesis: The Use of Psalm 16 in Acts 2," CBQ 43 (1981): 543–56.

9. On "Son of God" as a royal title in Mark, see Juel, *Messiah and Temple,* 108–14; *Mark* Augsburg Commentary on the New Testament (Minneapolis: Augsburg Books, 1990), 59–60. On the place of the title within Christian interpretation of the Old Testament, see Juel, *Messianic Exegesis,* 59–88.

also 2 Sam. 7:14). Although evidence from the Qumran Scrolls that "Son of God" could function as a messianic title in postbiblical Jewish circles is not absolutely convincing, it does demonstrate that 2 Samuel 7 (and probably Psalm 2) was regarded as a messianic oracle prior to Christianity, and that "son" was a designation for the Messiah-King used by God. Milik's now-famous fragment from cave 4 at least demonstrates that "Son of God" and "Son of the Most High God" were titles appropriate to royalty.[10]

All this suggests that one of the components in the title "Son of God" in Mark is royal. The prominent place of the title in the passion narrative, which tells the story of the trial and death of the "Messiah," the "King of the Jews" confirms the royal associations of the title. There may be additional components and associations. The demons know that Jesus is "the Son of God" and "the Son of the Most High God" (3:11; 5:7), but they never call him "Christ" (see, however, Luke 4:41, where the narrator views "Son of God" and "Christ" as synonymous). The use of the title "my Son" by God, however, in contexts where there are strong reminiscences of royal psalms (esp. Psalm 2 in Mark 1:11, 9:7) makes it likely that even the supernatural knowledge of Jesus' Sonship by demons should be understood as part of royal—that is, messianic—tradition.

The Baptism of Jesus

The passion narrative is constructed in such a way as to exploit the tension between messianic tradition and Jesus' messiahship.[11] The account of Jesus' baptism in the opening chapter of the Gospel plays on the same tension, in fact introducing it into the story. Central to appreciating the messianic overtones is the use of "my Son." The climax of the brief narrative is a *bat kol*, which employs biblical language. The most prominent image is from Psalm 2: "You are my son." As in the psalm, God personally calls the anointed one "my son." Messianic interpretation of Psalm 2 in pre-Christian tradition is nearly certain (see above).

It is also possible, as is well known, that the voice includes an allusion to Isa 42:1 (in nonseptuagintal form). Likewise conceivable is that the reference to a "beloved son" presumes an allusion to Genesis 22. There

---

10. The fragment was published by Joseph Fitzmyer in "The Contribution of Qumran Aramaic to the Study of the New Testament," *A Wandering Aramean*, SBLMS 25 (Missoula, Mont.: Scholars Press, 1979), 102–14.

11. See "A Context for Interpretation: From Papias to Perrin," chap. 2 in this volume.

is ample evidence in Paul (Rom. 8:32) that a link between Jesus and the "beloved son" of Abraham had been established prior to Mark; the mechanism for the link is even clear: the use of "seed" in 2 Sam. 7:12 and Gen. 22:18 is sufficient to argue that God's promise of a "seed" to David represented the fulfillment of his promise of a "seed" to Abraham, in whom all the nations would be blessed. A similar logic, predicated on the confession of Jesus as Messiah, led Jesus' followers to the "servant poems" in Isaiah as potentially messianic texts.[12] It is possible, in other words, that the voice at Jesus' baptism is formulated from scriptural passages that have become important features of Christian messianic exegetical tradition.

Likewise, the whole baptismal scene in Mark may be associated with scenes depicted both in the Testament of Levi (XVIII) and the Testament of Judah (XXIV). Separating Christian redaction from earlier narratives in the Testament of the Twelve Patriarchs is notoriously difficult on this point, but it is possible that the "confirmation" scene in which the heavens open and God pours out the Spirit on an eschatological office holder (in the Testament of the Twelve, either the priest or the king) was traditional, that is, pre-Christian.

The most striking feature of the baptismal story emerges from within the narrative setting, as we have seen in the third chapter. The more one knows about the background of the imagery in Mark, the more striking is the account. Jesus is introduced as the one greater than John who will baptize with the Holy Spirit—the Christ, Son of God. Yet when Jesus appears, it is not as the conquering warrior fitted with the appropriate trappings of a savior. The occasion for his confirmation by God and his anointing by the Spirit is John's Baptism, which is a washing for the forgiveness of sins. The tearing of the heavens, the descent of the Spirit, and the authoritative declaration of God are all fitting testimony to the stature of the promised deliverer. The setting is all wrong, however. Jesus should be among the mighty, in the great city that served David as his citadel, not among sinners who have come to repent of their sins.

The story opens with a great shock. The promised deliverer has been confirmed and anointed for his appointed tasks. Yet he looks nothing like what was expected; he is in the wrong place, associating with the wrong people. Jesus' career begins with a tension between what is expected of God and what God actually provides. As the narrative progresses, the tension increases rather than decreases. The ministry

12. See Juel, "The Servant-Christ," *Southwest Journal of Theology* 21 (1979): 7-22, and *Messianic Exegesis*, chap. 5.

that begins with a dramatic tearing of the heavens concludes with the tearing of the Temple curtain, as Jesus dies. He is condemned, ridiculed, and executed as "the King of the Jews" and as "the Christ, the Son of the Blessed One."

The baptismal scene introduces tensions into the narrative, which will be developed into a story that seeks to depict the reality of the "good news about Jesus Christ." And the tension central to the narrative arises from the difference between Jesus the Christ and traditional messianic speculation. The messianic associations of "Son of God" are central to this narrative strategy.

The Origin of Mark's Christology

One of the basic motifs in Mark's portrait of Jesus is the unprecedented nature of his ministry. He is the expected one, the one for whom God has prepared, the one whose career is in accordance with the Scriptures; yet his ministry does not fit established patterns or expectations. He associates with the wrong sorts of people, threatens tradition, and, at the climax of his ministry, is executed as a would-be king, rejected by the religious and political authorities, deserted by his followers, abandoned even by God. The tension is not a simple misperception but is in fact constitutive of the Gospel Mark knows. God's truth is disclosed only by way of confrontation with established tradition and human institutions. "Divine things" conflict with "human things" (Mark 8:33). "Fresh skins for new wine" stands as a useful summary of this feature of Mark's portrait of Jesus (2:22). For precisely this reason, irony is the only suitable means of narrating the climax of the story. Truth is not identical with appearance but must in some way be in tension with it. Jesus is a hero who does not look like a hero. Thus conventional ways of narrating stories about heroes are not sufficient as vehicles for the evangelists.

The tension between Jesus and the tradition is made concrete in the story in terms of his messianic office. The tension is between the royal title and his ignominious death on the cross. The inordinate amount of space devoted to the story of Jesus' trial and death testifies to the importance of this tension for understanding Jesus (and, for that matter, for understanding the will of God). Jesus must not simply die, but he must die as King. Scholars have frequently noted the prominence of biblical imagery in the passion narrative, particularly allusions to Psalms 22 and 69. The psalms, certainly in Mark, are enlisted in the task of telling the story of the death of Jesus, the King of the Jews. They do not provide an alternative view of Jesus (say, of Jesus as the paradigmatic righteous sufferer), nor do they provide an alternative derivation of Mark's Christology. As Martin Hengel has stated, the psalms are used to speak of Jesus as King.[13] Royal conceptions dominate Mark's passion narrative.

The origin of Mark's Christology cannot be found in post-biblical Jewish tradition, though it cannot be understood apart from such tradition. Jesus is indeed the Messiah—the only Messiah known by Jewish tradition prior to bar Kochba. But his career does not correspond to that of the promised Christ. Thus the adage formulated by Nils Dahl: the confession of Jesus as Messiah is the presupposition for New Testament Christology, but not its content.[14]

The origin of Mark's Christology can be traced first of all to the events that climaxed Jesus' ministry in Jerusalem—his arrest, trial, death, and vindication as Christ, the Son of the Blessed One, the King of the Jews. The events provided Mark, and the early Christian movement, with an agenda. What does it mean that the Messiah had to die? One alternative was to redraw Old Testament tradition until the scandal of the cross disappeared: "Was it not necessary that the Christ must suffer and on the third day rise?" The end product of such an approach is the Epistle of Barnabas and its apologetic. The alternative chosen by Mark (and Paul, and to a degree John) is to use the tension between Jesus the crucified Christ and messianic tradition as an interpretive key for understanding not only Jesus but God and the human situation. To overstate the matter somewhat, Mark used the tradition available to him to make sense of the career of one who died as King of the Jews, one whose vindication by God on the third day not only resulted in the tearing of the temple curtain and the ripping wide of the heavens but in a new conception of what royalty must mean.

13. Martin Hengel, *The Atonement,* trans. John Bowden (Philadelphia: Fortress Press, 1981), 41: "For Mark, the few psalms of suffering which illuminate individual features of the suffering and death of Jesus, like Psalms 22 and 69, are exclusively *messianic* psalms, such as Psalms 110 and 118." I have argued for such a messianic reading of the Psalms and have sketched a history of interpretation within early Christian circles in Juel, *Messianic Exegesis,* chap. 4.

Those who have sought to derive the Markan passion from the psalms without reference to messianic tradition include Carl Peddinghaus, "Die Entstehung der Leidensgeschichte: Eine traditionsgeschichtliche und historische Untersuchung des Werdens und Wachsens der erzählenden Passionstradition bis zum Entwurf des Markus," (Ph.D diss., University of Heidelberg, 1965), and Julius von Oswald, "Die Beziehungen zwischen Psalm 22 und dem vormarkinischen Passionsbericht," ZKT 101 (1979): 53–66. Their views are discussed in Matera, *The Kingship of Jesus,* 125–30.

14. The argument is developed in Dahl's *Jesus the Christ* (Minneapolis: Fortress Press, 1990).

The origin of Mark's Christology is to be sought in the history of Jesus of Nazareth, principally in the events that brought his career to an end and offered a whole new beginning. His Christology is focused there, in the cross of the one who died as "the King of the Jews." While other aspects of Jesus' history have shaped the narrative and other traditions that provide a matrix for Mark's story, none has had as decisive an impact on the shape of the narrative as the death of the would-be king.

The relationship between Jesus' messianic death and his nonmessianic career, so essential to Albert Schweitzer's construction of the life of Jesus, remains a central problem for theology. Interpreters have had difficulty holding the two features of the narrative together. Some have argued that Mark tells the story of Jesus' healings and exorcisms only to reject their relevance.[15] That seems unlikely. The crowds are not completely wrong in their assessment of Jesus as a prophetic (that is eschatological) figure, but they do not grasp the whole truth, which is focused in the confession of Jesus as the promised Christ—the Christ, of course, who died and was raised after three days. Others, like Brevard Childs, deny that Jesus' ministry was "radically nonmessianic," though they find little support for their denial either from Mark or from still-emerging scholarship on Jewish messianism.[16] Depictions of Jesus as Teacher or Friend of the Poor continue to appear that simply ignore the last third of the story. Such attempts have not managed to smooth over the transition from the one stage in Jesus' ministry to the next, perhaps because of stubborn historical particularities to which Mark's narrative gives testimony and by which it is constrained.

Mark's is not the only interpretation of Jesus' career. Luke is an example of attempts to integrate Jesus' ministry of preaching and healing into "messianic" categories. The move is apparent in the narrative in Luke 4 where the passage from Isaiah 61 about "anointing" provides a bridge between messianic and prophetic functions (Luke 4:18-19). Such movements led to apologetic writings like Justin's *Dialogue with Trypho* and the Epistle of Barnabas, where the differences between Jesus'

15. Such is the view, for example, of Theodore Weeden, *Traditions in Conflict* (Philadelphia: Fortress Press, 1971).

16. B. Childs, *Biblical Theology of the Old and New Testaments* (Minneapolis: Fortress Press, 1992), 228. See the evidence from the most recent scholarship on Messianism in James Charlesworth, ed., *The Messiah: Developments in Earliest Judaism and Christianity* (Minneapolis: Fortress Press, 1992). Although we have access today to a substantial body of Jewish literature Albert Schweitzer did not know, his insistence that Jesus' ministry of preaching and healing would have convinced no one that he was the Messiah remains convincing both historically and exegetically.

highly singular messianic career and the traditions of Israel are simply obliterated. Mark preserves the stark contrasts, which are reflected in a rhetorical strategy for which irony is crucial. In precisely this sense Mark's narrative remains the most historical, as many interpreters have suspected—but historical in a way that entails a theological claim: In the death of the King of the Jews we experience in the most profound way the great surprise that God had in store.

8

A Disquieting Silence:
The Matter of the Ending

No point in a story is as significant for appreciation and interpretation as its ending. That is surely the case in Mark's Gospel. The abrupt and unsatisfying conclusion has not surprisingly spawned a massive secondary literature—most of recent vintage, however. Interest in the ending became possible only with the publication of editions that relegated verses 9-20 to the footnotes. Until the great Alexandrian codices were known, few paid attention to the scattered references to a Gospel of Mark that lacked a proper conclusion. Further, only after a scholarly consensus had determined that Mark could no longer be read as Matthew's epitomizer could readers become fascinated—and troubled—by the mysterious anti-climax that forms the end of our Gospel: "So they went out and fled from the tomb, for terror and amazement had seized them; and they said nothing to anyone, for they were afraid" (Mark 16:8).

There are perhaps additional factors in the current fascination with the Markan ending. One is the willingness to read Mark as a narrative. When the text is broken down into component parts that are the focus of investigation, as among form critics, the strange conclusion can be explained more easily. The episode at the empty tomb may be read as an effort to explain why the story appeared so late in the tradition (the women never told anyone) or as an effort to put distance between the apostolic testimony and the resurrection from the empty tomb. Such explanations require detaching the verses from their narrative setting and proposing another, hypothetical *Sitz im Leben* in the context of which the snippet is to be understood. The verses sound rather different as the conclusion of a narrative. Any who have been present at one of David Rhoads's "presentations" of Mark can testify to the uneasiness in the audience when the last words are spoken—even in an audience of sophisticates who know in advance how the narrative will end.[1]

There is much ground to cover in any study of Mark's ending. Fortunately the whole field need not be replowed. Andrew Lincoln's fine piece in the Journal of Biblical Literature has made it unnecessary to review all of the research.[2] His analysis of current studies, his examination of words for "terror" and "amazement" in Mark, his brief review of evidence for ending a sentence with *gar*—such matters require little additional comment. I prefer to confine my study to the experience of the ending and to ask if criticism has any role at all to play in commending a particular experience of the Gospel's ending—and thus of the narrative as a whole.

While we might speak of a scholarly consensus regarding the ending of Mark, there is surely no consensus regarding its interpretation. In fact, there is still reluctance among interpreters to settle with 16:8 as the conclusion of the Gospel. That reluctance gives evidence of a feature of public imagination well analyzed by Frank Kermode in his *The Sense of an Ending*:[3] people do not tolerate unfinished stories easily. Consider the comment in the Oxford Study Bible:

> Nothing is certainly known either about how this Gospel originally ended or about the origin of vv. 9-20, which cannot have been part of the original text of Mark . . . Though it is possible that the compiler(!) of the Gospel intended this abrupt ending, one can find hints that he intended to describe events after the resurrection.[4]

Such speculation is a clear refusal to read the work as it appears in the best-attested readings; it is very much of the same order as the endings tacked on by ancient copyists who could not tolerate a Gospel that ended with frightened women. Interpretation of the ending will necessarily involve scrutiny of our own needs as readers—in this case,

1. David Rhoads's presentation of Mark's Gospel has been prepared on videocassette by the LITE continuing education center at Trinity Lutheran Seminary in Columbus, Ohio. Because Rhoads works from modern editions of Mark, his performance differs from the more famous presentation of Mark by Alec McGowan, who works from the KJV and ends with 16:20 ("Amen"). See D. Rhoads and D. Michie, *Mark as Story* (Philadelphia: Fortress Press, 1982).

2. Andrew Lincoln, "The Promise and the Failure—Mark 16:7,8," JBL 108 (1989): 283–300.

3. Frank Kermode, *The Sense of an Ending: Studies in the Theory of Fiction* (London: Oxford Univ. Press, 1966).

4. *The New Oxford Annotated Bible* (New York: Oxford Univ. Press, 1977), 1238.

suspicion about interpretations that cannot reckon with "for they were afraid" as a conclusion of a Gospel.

Perhaps it should be stated explicitly that the Gospel according to Mark that we are interpreting ends with 16:8. That is not the Gospel read by most generations of Christians. Modern text-critics and editors believe there are good reasons to omit the "spurious" endings that for centuries constituted the conclusion of the church's Gospel. While it would be satisfying to describe our printed text as the original version of Mark's Gospel, greater modesty is advisable. The task of text-critics is to establish the "best" text that can then be printed. Through judicious selections among the alternatives available in the manuscript tradition, scholars can establish a version of the Gospel for which the best arguments can be advanced.[5] The plausibility of text-critical arguments can be tested through a variety of means, both historical and literary. Interpretations that demonstrate coherence in a version of Mark ending with 16:8 add probability to arguments that deal with manuscripts of the Gospel. The reconstruction of an implied audience for whom such a narrative would be appropriate likewise adds plausibility. For example, the abrupt ending makes more sense if the Gospel is addressed to believers than if it were intended as missionary propaganda. Such an implied audience would have to be tested by interpretation of the remainder of the Gospel as well as by historical arguments: Could such an audience have existed in early Christianity as we know it? What setting and function for a narrative might we suggest within such a religious community? The point is that even decisions about what will be printed as the Bible will require arguments that proceed according to agreed-upon ground rules. For our purposes, it is enough to note that the majority of experts in the field of Gospel criticism believe there are good reasons to print as the Gospel according to Mark a version that ends with 16:8. Because that is the case, the format chosen for printing the Gospel ought to make it crystal clear to readers that Mark ends at 16:8. The use of paragraph headings like "longer ending" and "shorter ending," and the use of double brackets in both the Greek New Testament and in the NRSV, is an unfortunate compromise that is more confusing than helpful. One suspects that the use of critical symbols rather than using different size print for alternative versions of the Markan ending represents equivocation on the part of translation committees. The stubborn refusal of commentators to accept sound text-critical arguments in their interpretation of Mark and the continuing

5. For a careful analysis of the logic of text-critical arguments, see Humphrey Palmer, *The Logic of Gospel Criticism* (New York: St. Martin's Press, 1968), 55–111.

creation of hypothetical conclusions say more about commentators than about Mark.

Comments by Brevard Childs in his singular *Introduction to the New Testament as Canon* bear at least some passing comment in this regard.[6] Childs argues that the alternative ending ought to be read as part of the canonical Mark. His concern arises in part from acknowledgment that the Mark known to most generations of Christians included verses after 16:8. Childs seeks a compromise interpretation. He argues that verses 9-20 should be read as the canonical reading of Mark because the verses employ bits and pieces from the remaining three Gospels. The verses, he believes, seek to prevent aberrant readings of Mark that might suggest undue differences from the other Gospels. There is no real problem with reading the verses as part of the canonical Mark because "the same theological point made by the original ending has been retained, but extended," namely the disciples' unbelief in the face of the resurrection.

Such an argument is interesting, but it largely misses the point. Endings are important more for what they do than for the ideas they include. Verse 8 does something radically different as an ending than does verse 20, something that shapes the whole experience of reading the Gospel. It is the whole impact of the canonical Mark that ought to be of interest to readers, not simply the ideas extracted from it. If we agree that the version of the Gospel in the manuscript tradition with the strongest claim to logical priority deserves to be printed in Bibles, it is this version—ending with verse 8—that will function as canon. It is the function of this ending that I wish to explore, with the help of Kermode.

The Experience of the Ending

An ending does things. It can achieve closure, pulling together loose threads from a story, or it can resist closure, refusing to answer burning questions posed in the course of the narrative. Kermode's analysis both in *The Sense of an Ending* and *The Genesis of Secrecy*[7] explores that experience of closure in narrative. His analysis of the wide range of interplay between reader and story necessarily involves attention to the

---

6. B. Childs, *Introduction to the New Testament as Canon* (Philadelphia: Fortress Press, 1985), 94–95. It will be of interest later that, according to Childs, the canonical reading of Mark in verses 9-20 clearly rules out a positive interpretation of the terror and amazement of the women at the tomb.

7. Kermode, *Sense of an Ending,* and *Genesis of Secrecy* (Cambridge, Mass.: Harvard Univ. Press, 1979).

expectations and needs of readers. We write and read stories, he insists, because we must. Stories, and the interpretation of stories, represent a way of dealing with a confusing and "unfollowable" world. His analysis does not seek to replace the reading of stories with something else but to prepare readers to be a more responsive and critical audience. As is the case with other art forms, the Gospel must be experienced; study prepares hearers to listen for themes, for invention, for irony and surprise.

Study is necessary because we are not obviously good readers. In a culture suspicious of words, students need to be coaxed to give them a try. Further, readers must develop a sense of expectancy, learning what to look for and where to find clues. Preparing readers for engaging a narrative with an image or a suggestion makes them susceptible to ideological and institutional biases, of course. Yet without such biases, communication would be impossible. There must be some rules of communication, some sense of what to expect. Kermode has no illusions about objective readings of narratives, but he does seek to prepare critical readers by alerting them to institutional biases. Given the importance of the Bible to the life of the church as well as to the academic community, it is hardly surprising that representatives of such institutions carefully protect their investments by regulating interpretation. We study to see more deeply and to overcome confusion and bewilderment in our reading. Study can, however, protect vested interests and permit personal satisfaction at the expense of what is read.

The ending of Mark's Gospel provides a particular challenge to interpreters. The reason is its failure to resolve the tensions in the story and to provide some sense of closure that seems appropriate to "good news about Jesus Christ." Taken at face value, the concluding verse constitutes a disappointing end: nothing comes of the whole enterprise because the women do not speak. Few interpreters will accept such a reading of the Gospel, of course. For the less sophisticated readers who are familiar with Matthew, Luke, and John, it is difficult even to hear Mark. Endings are automatically supplied, probably much like the familiar "longer ending" printed in the NRSV. Imagination does not even attend to the discord. The same is true of commentators—sensible Bible readers who insist that disappointment in the performance of the women is the result of misunderstanding. One senses a kind of desperation in the otherwise fine study of Schüssler Fiorenza who must at all costs find heroism in the women at the tomb.[8] A similar defensiveness seems

8. Elizabeth Schüssler Fiorenza, *In Memory of Her: A Feminist Theological Reconstruction of Christian Origins* (New York: Crossroad, 1983), 316–23.

to dominate those who argue that the *tromos* and *ekstasis* that take hold of the women at the conclusion of the story, and the fear that drives them to flee, are positive emotions.[9] At least at first reading, the failure of the women to spread the good news is hardly commendable, and the fear with which they are possessed is little different from the fear that plagues the disciples throughout the story. Our need to overcome this experience of disappointment is the primary motor that drives interpretation.

There may well be good reasons to read the ending as hopeful, but that hopeful reading cannot be purchased at the expense of Mark's narrative. I do not wish to belabor the point, but the history of the Markan ending in manuscript and commentary betrays an unwillingness or inability to take the disappointment seriously. It is as if there is an emotional barrier that must be broken through if the Gospel is to be heard.

In the midst of a discussion of Mark 16 in class, in which young interpreters were finding one reason after another for regarding the Gospel's ending as upbeat, one student raised her hand and said, "I read the ending over several times last evening in preparation for class. I thought about it—and I cried." There was something about that experience—an honesty, an ability to read with defenses down, a willingness to acknowledge disappointment—that changed the course of the class discussion.

One of Kermode's great contributions is a willingness to entertain the possibility that there are no satisfying endings—in Mark or in life. Intrigued by the tension between literary form and the formlessness of

---

9. See the brief discussion by Lincoln, "Promise and Failure," 286.
More compelling than most are the comments of John Donahue in his *The Gospel in Parable* (Philadelphia: Fortress Press, 1988), 196–97:

> Mark's theology of fear and wonder emerges especially in the resurrection account (16:5,8) and in the jarring ending of the Gospel, "They were afraid" (16:8). This motif, which throughout the Gospel establishes rapport with the readers and dictates how they should respond to Jesus, now becomes a symbolic reaction to the gospel as a whole. Mark's readers are left not even with the assurance of a resurrection vision but simply with numinous fear in the face of a divine promise.
>
> These reactions of wonder and surprise accompany the revelation of God in Jesus, and they signify the power of this revelation to unsettle and challenge human existence. At the same time, this wonder is fascinating and attracting; it invites people to confront mystery. Such motifs call for a parabolic reading of Mark: for an approach to Mark's Jesus with a sense of wonder, awe, and holy fear.

Yet even here, "fear" is understood not as incapacitating and blinding but as opening and inviting. This too easily resolves the tension on which the Gospel plays.

the world explored by such writers as Kafka, aware of the power of language and story to satisfy and to console, and of the deep human need for satisfaction and consolation, he is well-suited as a critic to examine the experience of reading Mark's Gospel. He is particularly adept at unmasking fraudulent readings that refuse to take Mark's narrative seriously—readings that, more often than not, are proposed by representatives of institutions with considerable investment in interpretation (for example, the church or the learned community); his distaste for Jeremias's approach to the parables is particularly striking, and his critique effective.[10] His critical reflections suggest certain questions are central, and I would like to deal with them. Does the Gospel make sense in light of the ending, or is it nonsense? Are there ways to offer good reasons for one reading or another? And finally, do the troubling verses give reason to look forward to an ending that is inviting and hopeful?

As with many other students of Mark, I wish to focus on the last two verses. In his study, Lincoln characterizes the experience of verse 7 and 8 in terms of promise and failure.[11] Focusing on the response of the reader, I would speak rather of hope and disappointment. Much is invested in a reading of these two verses and their bearing on the argument that the Gospel seeks to make.

"As he told you": The Argument for a Satisfying Ending

The astonished women do not find Jesus in the tomb, as they had expected. Instead, they encounter a young man dressed in a white robe. While several interpretations of this figure are possible, we are probably to think of a heavenly messenger. That is surely the way Matthew and Luke heard the term, and both eliminate any possible ambiguity with their embellishments.

The women are appropriately terrified. The herald offers customary assurance that they need not be alarmed. He points to the obvious: Jesus is no longer in the tomb. Hoping to achieve some sort of closure to Jesus' unpredictable career by anointing his body for burial, the women are stunned by one more surprise: Jesus cannot be confined by the tomb any more than by the hopes of his followers or the designs of his enemies. The grave clothes have been shed; Jesus is out of the tomb, on the loose.

10. Kermode, *Genesis of Secrecy*, chap. 2.
11. Lincoln, "Promise and Failure," 290–92.

Perhaps the most important feature of the herald's announcement is the closing: "Go, tell his disciples and Peter, that he is going ahead of you to Galilee; there you will see him, just as he told you" (Mark 16:7). "As he told you." The reminder takes on considerable significance when the verse is read within the context of the whole story. Jesus has, in fact, made such a promise. The little collection of prophecies recounted just prior to Jesus' arrest (14:28-30) include a scriptural reference to Zechariah ("I will strike the shepherd, and the sheep will be scattered"), a detailed forecast of Peter's denial, and the promise that he will precede his disciples to Galilee after his resurrection.

The prophecy of Peter's denial is quite precise. The rhyming couplet (nicely captured in the KJV's "Before the cock crows twice, you will deny me thrice") is repeated by the narrator at the conclusion of Peter's trial: "Then Peter remembered that Jesus had said to him, 'Before the cock crows twice, you will deny me three times.' And he broke down and wept" (14:72). Jesus' prophecy is fulfilled to the letter. Even the detail about the second crowing of the cock is noted carefully (14:72). And while this unlikely scenario of Peter's collapse is being played out in the courtyard of the high priest's house, inside Jesus is being taunted to prophesy by the servants of those who have condemned him to death. Jesus' prophecies, we are reminded, do indeed come to pass, a detail that offers a glimpse into the deeper dimensions of the narrative Mark recounts.

"As he told you." The specific forecast of Jesus' resurrection in 14:28 is only one of many statements Jesus makes about what will happen. Three times Jesus formally predicts his death—and his resurrection (8:31; 9:31; 10:33), predictions that are given the added force of necessity (*dei*, 8:31; 9:11). That "necessity" has to do with the will of God recorded in the Scriptures: "The stone that the builders rejected has become the cornerstone" (12:10, quoting Psalm 118:22); "The Son of Man goes as it has been written of him" (14:21); "But let the scriptures be fulfilled" (14:49).

The collection of parables in chapter four offers figurative predictions of what lies beyond the boundaries of the narrative: planting, despite obstacles, will result in harvests; a tiny seed will produce a full-grown bush. "There is nothing hidden, except to be disclosed," Jesus promises (4:21-24). Jesus speaks to his disciples of the inevitable onset of birth pangs that precede the coming of the Son of Man with the clouds of heaven (13:8). He promises that the Gospel must be preached to all nations (13:10). James and John are told that they will indeed share in his cup and baptism (10:39). His numerous promises have important functions in the narrative. They foreshadow; they give to the story a sense of direction and purpose; they point to what lies beyond the story. Promises that are fulfilled provide a basis for confidence that others will be. His glimpses of what lies ahead create a momentum that drives readers beyond the ending into the period beyond the story. "There you will see him, just as he told you" (16:7). The narrative offers reason to believe that what Jesus promises will take place.

The announcement from the empty tomb that Jesus has been raised— as he said he would be—thus opens a gateway to the future. The disciples will surely see him. Whatever the obstacles, the harvest will come; the tiny seed will grow into a shrub large enough to provide nesting places for the birds; at the end of the birth pangs one can expect new life. There is reason to recount Jesus' story as good news because the reader can believe what Jesus "told you." That, at least, is one argument the narrative offers. There is someone to tell the story, itself an indication that it did not end with fearful women.

"They said nothing to anyone": The Argument for an Unsatisfying Ending

Were Mark's Gospel to end with 16:7, there would be far less interest in chapter 16, and in Mark's Gospel. It does not. As readers, we have been led to expect something other than verse 8. When Jesus enjoins his bewildered disciples to say nothing about the events on the Mount of Transfiguration, he suggests a limit to their silence: "until after the Son of Man had risen from the dead" (9:9). That Peter, James, and John understand nothing of what Jesus is saying to them only heightens interest in what is to come. Expectations are planted in readers. There will be a time of openness, a time for disclosing and speaking (4:21-22). There is good reason to believe that Jesus' resurrection will mark the transition from one time to another. Yet, in the narrative world at least, that is not to be.

Neither the stirring words of the divine messenger nor the empty tomb succeed in making evangelists of the women who have come to do their duty to a corpse. Like the disciples (14:50) and the young man seized in the garden (14:52), they flee (the word *pheugo* appears also in 5:14 to describe the actions of the swineherds in the land of the Gerasenes, and in Jesus' warnings in 13:14). The reason, we are told, is that "trembling and ecstasy held them fast." They say nothing to anyone—they were afraid, you see (Kermode's paraphrase). The terrible irony is that now is the time to speak. The tomb is empty; the crucified King is alive, vindicated by God, as he said he would be. What is hidden may now come to light (4:21-22); the disciples can tell secret things they were commanded to withhold now that Jesus has risen from the dead (9:9). The faithful women have the opportunity to do what the men could not. And they fail. They flee, just as the men—because they are afraid.

Arguments that the trembling, ecstasy, and fear are positive terms, appropriate to the presence of the divine, seem akin to Matthew's reading of Mark: "So they left the tomb quickly with fear and great joy, and ran to tell his disciples" (Matt. 28:8). Slight changes in wording yield a very different sense; "They left quickly with fear and great joy" is worlds away from "They fled . . . for they were afraid." Their flight and their inability to do as they were commanded remains.

Insisting that the women told no one "for the present" has little support in the narrative. The story has offered no reason to place confidence in any insiders. While the women at least do their duty, like the disciples of John the Baptist did when they claimed his body and laid it in a tomb (6:29), they do not anticipate a miracle. They come fully expecting to find a corpse. Auerbach's analysis of Peter's performance seems an appropriate reading of the women's performance as well: They come closer to genuine greatness than the other disciples, only to fall further.[12] Even in the face of an empty tomb and testimony to Jesus' resurrection, the women cannot believe in such a way as to perform the most basic task of disciples: testimony. They tell no one the good news. They flee, and we are left to imagine what became of them, as we are left to imagine the fate of Judas, and the naked young man, and Peter, and the Twelve.

If Mark argues that there is reason to believe the gospel will be preached to the nations, the narrative simultaneously undercuts any confidence in the performance of characters without whom the whole enterprise seems lost.

Mark's Gospel ends with both hope and disappointment. The relationship between the last two verses embodies the critical tension in the story between blindness and insight, concealment and openness, silence and proclamation. The tension is not resolved. Why is this so? To what end does the tension lead? It is to that question we now turn, with the help of Kermode.

---

12. Eric Auerbach, *Mimesis,* trans. W. Trask (Princeton: Princeton Univ. Press, 1953), 24–49. Borrowing a term from Harnack, Auerbach refers to the "pendulation" in such characters.

Doors

Kermode's study of endings is driven by a conviction that stories are essential to life as a way of making sense of an unfollowable world. His fascination with Kafka and other existentialist writers arises from the perceived tension between reality and form. Human beings create order and form, so the argument goes, as a necessary response to the form-lessness and meaningless of the world. To make that argument, to be sure, writers like Kafka must employ traditional forms that purport to represent reality—narrative forms that feature genuine endings—but they do so in such fashion as to create doubts about our ability to make contact with some fundamental order. Kermode senses that there is something hollow, even untruthful, about imitations of a coherent and purposeful reality, however noble the motivations of artists and however necessary their fictions to our sense of well-being. Art imposes order on what is beyond our ordering; it attempts to grasp what is beyond our reach. While one can imagine some ultimate plan or design, it remains out there, unfollowable. Art can achieve meaning, therefore, only at the expense of truth.

Art is most interesting, therefore, for what it tells us about ourselves. It arises from our need for order, a need that seems basic to the species. In analyzing stories, Kermode entertains, with structuralists, the possibility that basic paradigms underlie all narrative:

> Now presumably it is true, in spite of all possible cultural and historical variations, that the paradigm will correspond, the more fully as one approaches a condition of absolute simplicity, to some basic human "set," biological or psychological. Right down at the root, they must correspond to a basic human need, they must make sense, give comfort.[13]

If that is so, the closing verses of the Gospel are all the more intriguing, for the initial experience of the ending suggests that it does not fit the paradigm. The conclusion does little to offer a sense of an ending without which the story makes no sense.

> Mark's book began with a trumpet call: "This is the beginning of the gospel of Jesus Christ, the Son of God" (1:1). It ends with this faint whisper of timid women. There are, as I say, ways of ending narratives that are not manifest and simple devices of closure, not the distribution of rewards, punishments, hands in marriage, of whatever satisfies our simpler intuitions of completeness. But this one seems at first sight wholly

13. Kermode, *Sense of an Ending,* 43–44.

counter-intuitive, as it must have to the man who added the twelve verses
we now have at the end.[14]

Part of the difficulty in conversing with Kermode is that he offers
no sustained interpretation of Mark, because that is not his purpose.
He offers only hints. He seems willing to entertain the possibility that
the ending does "make sense," although such an interpretation is not
obvious. He seems most disposed to the imaginative work of people
like Austin Farrer, whose creative exploration of literary patterns places
him outside the usual guild of Markan scholars.[15] Offering his interpretation of the Markan ending would accomplish little, however, because his major concern is to bring naive readers face to face with the
genuinely enigmatic character of Mark: The Gospel generates secrecy,
not just secrets. While it holds out the prospect that readers can become
insiders, the possibility turns out to be illusory. Placed in this hermeneutical bind, interpreters with institutional allegiances and an investment in coherence and meaning are forced to employ cunning and
violence to extract what they need from the text. The experience of
disappointment must at all costs be overcome.[16]

Kermode is by no means exempt from such institutional allegiances,
of course, and he is capable of employing cunning and violence to
achieve his own ends, as he would readily admit. Few would accuse
him of violence, but we should not fail to appreciate the single most
remarkable act of cunning in his approach to Mark: the selection of
Kafka's parable as a controlling image. Here is Kermode's version of
the parable:

> A man comes and begs for admittance to the Law, but is kept out by a
> doorkeeper, the first of a long succession of doorkeepers, of aspect even
> more terrible, who will keep the man out should the first one fail to do
> so. The man, who had assumed that the Law was open to all, is surprised
> to discover the existence of this arrangement. But he waits outside the
> door, sitting year after year on his stool, and conversing with the door-
> keeper, whom he bribes, though without success.
>
> Eventually, when he is old and near death, the man observes an im-
> mortal radiance streaming from the door. As he dies, he asks the door-
> keeper how it is that he alone has come to this entrance to seek admittance
> to the Law. The answer is, "This door was intended only for you. Now
> I am going to shut it." The outsider, though someone had "intended"
> to let him in, or anyway provided a door for him, remained outside.[17]

14. Kermode, *Genesis of Secrecy,* 68.
15. Austin Farrer, *A Study in Mark* (London, 1951).
16. Kermode, *Genesis of Secrecy,* 71–72 (among many examples).
17. *Ibid.,* 27–28.

The parable, introduced in chapter 2, moves in and out of the study and provides Kermode with the dramatic conclusion to his book:

> This is the way we satisfy ourselves with explanations of the unfollowable world—as if it were a structured narrative, of which more might always be said by trained readers of it, by insiders. World and book, it may be, are hopelessly plural, endlessly disappointing; we stand alone before them, aware of their arbitrariness and impenetrability, knowing that they may be narratives only because of our impudent intervention, and susceptible of interpretation only by our hermetic tricks. Hot for secrets, our only conversation may be with guardians who know less and see less than we can; and our sole hope and pleasure is in the perception of a momentary radiance, before the door of disappointment is finally shut on us.[18]

The image gives to Kermode's work a genuine ending; it makes sense of his study and his passion to explore the whole matter of secrecy. Mark, Kermode argues, has no ending in the sense that it can be grasped by any particular reading. The enigmatic conclusion becomes symptomatic of a deeper hermeneutical problem: There can be no ending. Mark will continue to generate new readings. Readings will always be particular—and limited. If ultimate reality is inaccessible to us, as Kafka's parable argues, if the most we can hope for is a glimpse at best, if we are and always will be outsiders, then the lesson for scriptural interpreters seems to be that they would do best to remain satisfied with questions of meaning, never to claim too much for an interpretation, and to bracket out questions of truth from interpretation.

In an important sense, this is quite different from the argument made by Mark's narrative. Consider the differences between Mark's Gospel and Kafka's parable. As in Kafka's work, Mark's narrative generates expectancy. Jesus' parables speak of seed time and harvest, of small seeds and large shrubs. Apparently insignificant beginnings drive toward magnificent conclusions, despite obstacles that stand in the way. Jesus daringly labels the tribulations that lie ahead birth pangs; creation groans in anticipation of what will come. He promises his resurrection and his return with the clouds, when he will gather his elect from the four winds. As in Kafka's parable, there is also disappointment. The world into which the reader is invited is one in which people fail. Longed for resolutions do not occur. Loose ends are not tied up. It is as Jesus says: "the end is still to come" (13:7).

The difference between Mark's story and Kafka's has to do with closure. There is genuine closure in Kafka's parable. The door is shut

18. *Ibid.*, 145.

as the old man dies, and with it the possibility of insight. There is no more waiting. The message is clear: We have been permanently shut out. Meaningfulness, such as it exists, is accessible to us only as we are able to supply it. We remain outside the door, forever.

Mark's Gospel forbids precisely that closure. There is no stone at the mouth of the tomb. Jesus is out, on the loose, on the same side of the door as the women and the readers. The story cannot contain the promises. Its massive investment in the reliability of Jesus' words becomes a down payment on a genuine future. Caught up in the narrative's momentum, the last words of the messenger at the tomb impel the reader beyond the confines of the narrative: "There you will see him, as he told you" (16:7). There will be enlightenment and speaking; the disciples will somehow play the role for which they have been chosen.

The door is a powerful image. It can open to possibilities or it can bar entrance. It is precisely the possiblity of opening that makes the conclusion of Kafka's parable—the shutting door—so devastating. Kermode has not attended to such imagery in Mark. The doors in Mark's Gospel are emphatically open: The curtain of the Temple is rent asunder (as is the curtain of the heavens at Jesus' baptism) and the stone is rolled back from the tomb. There is surely disappointment as the women flee, dashing hopes that at least one group of followers will prove faithful. But Jesus is out of the tomb; God is no longer safely behind the curtain. To hear in Mark's elusive ending the strains of Handel's "Halleluia Chorus" would require drowning out the music being performed. But to insist that the discordant ending offers no promise of resolution whatever is to do equal violence to the story. Jesus has promised an end. That end is not yet, but the story gives good reasons to remain hopeful even in the face of disappointment. The possibilities of eventual enlightenment for the reader remain in the hands of the divine actor who will not be shut in—or out.

Kermode's analysis clearly exposes the human need for closure, structure, and control. One can argue theologically from the same premises that interpretation can become a way of defending ourselves against truths that make a claim on us. The argument of Kafka's parables is that whatever truth exists is inaccessible to us—except the truth that we are alone in the face of the impenetrable. Mark's Gospel—and, we might add, the whole Christian tradition—argues that our lack of enlightenment and bondage arise from attempts to box God in or out of experience. All such attempts come to grief in the resurrection of Jesus. He cannot be confined by the tomb or limited by death. In Jesus' ministry, God tears away barriers that afforded protection in the past. God cannot be kept at arm's length. Such a possibility that light dawns even on those who inhabit the realm of darkness is disquieting; it means there is no refuge for the cynical any more than for the naive.

The possibility that the future is open may send interpreters scurrying to the ramparts, fearful for their lives. There is reason for sobriety. The Gospel offers little promise that we have control of our destiny. Interpretation only makes matters worse. The deeper into the narrative we delve, the less control we are promised. If the unresolved ending offers promise, it is surely not because we are encouraged to believe that we can do better than the disciples or the women. We do not "have" Jesus even at the end of the story, and there is no guarantee that we can wrest a promise from him or lock him safely away by hermeneutical tricks. Here Kermode is surely correct. But perhaps that is just where the promise resides. "There you will see him, as he told you." Jesus has promised an encounter with him against which there is no assured defense. God will be put off neither by our failures, or infidelity, nor by our most sophisticated interpretive schemes. And if this "good news about Jesus Christ" is God's work within the intimate realm of human speech, there is reason to hope that our defenses will finally prove insufficient and that we will not have the last word. The history of the Markan ending is perhaps ample testimony that this "gospel" will not easily be dismissed.

One's choice of images by which to open readers to a narrative can be a matter of cunning and violence. A choice is necessary nevertheless, and I believe there are good reasons for choosing an image other than the closed door in Kafka's parable. Given Kermode's fascination with John's Apocalypse, I would suggest this one:

> "These are the words of the holy one, the true one,
>   who has the key of David,
>   who opens and no one will shut,
>   who shuts and no one opens: . . .

Look, I have set before you an open door, which no one is able to shut." (Rev. 3:7-8)

9

Becoming an Audience: Reading and the Constraints of the Particular

Every rhetorical act discloses three characters, according to Aristotle: the character of the speaker (*ethos*), of the speech (*logos*), and of the audience (*pathos*). Not surprisingly, studies of Mark usually include some reflection on author and audience as well as on the story. The three are related and, as Aristotle argues, in rhetorical terms. That means simply that literature, as all human communication, is rhetorical: It seeks to move an audience, to change minds or feelings. We should expect that with something as intentional as a gospel narrative or letter, the rhetorical features should be identifiable. By features I do not mean first of all the whole taxonomy by which students of rhetoric order their study of literature, although the technical discussion is not excluded. I mean something more elementary: In reading a piece of literature, we become aware of an author pulling the strings behind the scenes; we are aware of the story; and we are—intentionally or not—an audience of some sort.

This last clause requires some comment. One might say that as critical readers we become aware of an audience. That is the way most studies proceed. Interest in audience is usually cast in historical terms. Phrases like "Markan Community" have been used largely to describe another audience at another time.[1] While most professional students of the New

1. Howard Kee's *Community of the New Age: Studies in Mark's Gospel* (Philadelphia: Westminster Press, 1977) is typical of such studies. Kee's creative use of historical and sociological material to profile the group out of which Mark's Gospel arises and for whom

Testament undertake their work to enhance the appreciation or correct impressions of their contemporaries, it is not always clear in what ways their work contributes to the building of a more sensitive and appreciative audience capable of being addressed by a piece of literature. In his now-famous essay on biblical interpretation, Krister Stendahl argued that by describing what the Bible meant to its contemporaries, scholars can revolutionize the way modern audiences understand what it means. He was correct. The problem, as a generation of scholars has observed, is that the revolution has rendered the Bible meaningful to many contemporary students only as a piece of antiquity. Historical study has a way of creating a gulf between present readers and the text, which is difficult to bridge.

The task of interpretation is to determine what a text means. If the Gospels are narrative arguments intended to change minds and shape experiences of God and the world, we are the readers who should be engaged by the arguments. Our study of the Markan Community as a literary or historical construct should serve to prepare us and our contemporaries for a richer and more imaginative hearing of the Gospel as a word for us.[2] By means of our interpretation, we can become or can shape the Markan Community in the only sense that matters.

Critical study has an important role to play in the enterprise of hearing the Gospel. Communication across barriers of time and cultures requires considerable imagination, for others are not exactly like us. Mark's audience heard Greek in a way we never will, however practiced we become. They knew things we will never know, things that could make sense of what is for us nonsense. For this reason our confidence in finding a word for ourselves is tempered by a recognition of what work must be done if we are to become a decent audience. Respect for the otherness of the New Testament should involve some schooling in the basic competencies presumed by New Testament authors. While contemporary readers are capable of imaginative engagement with Mark's Gospel without much schooling, the way the narrative operates in the imagination depends upon certain constraints and clues.

---

it is written is in service of a historical task. While the implications of such a reconstruction of a past audience for contemporary appreciation of the Gospel's claims may occasionally shine through, Kee's reading remains at a distance, describing how things were at a particular time and place.

2. Vernon Robbins's *Jesus the Teacher. A Socio-Rhetorical Interpretation of Mark* (Philadelphia: Fortress Press, 1984) highlights the rhetorical character of narrative, although his study locates the work in another culture, at another time and place. The Gospel's arguments are for a specific community. To what extent they address us is not explored in the book, although one may get hints of the author's own ethical concerns throughout his work.

Some examples of how knowledge can enrich or alter our reading come quickly to mind. It has been customary in some circles to understand the Pharisees in Mark as stock villains. Careful attention to the Gospel ought to have called such a caricature into question, at least to some degree: The Pharisees plot how to destroy Jesus (3:6), but their only role in the climactic scenes where Jesus' fate is sealed is to ask a loaded question on behalf of religious officials ("They sent to him some Pharisees and some Herodians . . .," 12:13). In Mark's story, they are not responsible for Jesus' arrest and execution. Further, the issues in which they are interested—sabbath observance, dietary laws, purity—are far from trivial. A more appreciative reading of Jewish history makes the Pharisees far more interesting characters in the story than earlier generations of New Testament readers have presumed. Committed as they are to the orderliness of creation as defined by the Law in a pagan world hostile to Jewish tradition, these ancestors of rabbinic Judaism are not at all unsympathetic characters. Responsible members of our own society troubled by the corrosive effect of sentimental religiosity on responsibility and morals should have some sympathy with their concerns. New conversations about the nature of the Jewish community in the first century—conversations that reflect present experience as well as new data—make the drama Mark narrates more interesting and profound.[3]

The role of critical study will depend, of course, on the larger hermeneutical enterprise. If what the Bible means is understood in propositional terms, audience will have little role to play in the interpretive enterprise. Interpretation will consist in ferreting out religiously significant facts on which to build some construct. If meaning is understood in terms of impact on an audience—in other words, if the Bible is understood in rhetorical terms as aimed at changing minds and shaping opinions—audience will be a more significant consideration. It is important then to ask what mind we are interested in. Form critics committed to constructing the *Sitz im Leben* of traditions and the mind of the community behind the Gospels will be interested in audience in a rather different way than those who focus interest on the mind of the community for whom Mark's Gospel was written. And such study may be quite different from that of readers interested in the world in front of the text and its power to persuade and to change the minds of contemporary audiences. While historical study is significant for the

---

3. Current appreciation of what used to be termed late Judaism (and is now termed in many quarters early Judaism) is surely shaped by differences in the current religious and social setting within which the Bible is read, itself a reality shaped by historical forces.

narrative-oriented reader, it will not be the primary mode of interpretation. Reconstructing the history behind the text or the mind of an author or community will not do what interpretation must do, namely to facilitate engagement with the Bible as a work that makes claims on us. If interpreters ought to be concerned principally with the latter, one of the tasks must be to understand the role of historical reconstruction.[4]

The First-Century Markan Community

It is instructive to observe how various interpreters have dealt with the matter of audience. Few will disagree that the Gospels presume an audience. While that may not be as clear as in the case of Paul's correspondence with the church at Corinth or the churches in Galatia, the narratives presume a group with particular concerns and investments. Luke identifies at least one reader, Theophilus, and presumes some familiarity with other versions of Jesus' story ("many" in 1:1) as well as a prior investment in the story of Jesus and the church ("the things about which you have been instructed," 1:4).

Interpreting the story depends upon a sense of that audience. W. D. Davies's work on the Sermon on the Mount in Matthew works with an historical construct, "Jamnia," over against which Christian rabbis offer their own version of halakah.[5] Ray Brown and Louis Martyn locate the Johannine community in a setting where, following the destruction of the Temple in 70 C.E., purgings and redrawing of boundaries are occurring.[6] The alternative profiles of the Lukan church drawn by Hans Conzelmann and Ernst Haenchen on the one hand and Jacob Jervell on the other result in dramatically different readings of Luke-Acts.[7]

4. For a preliminary sorting out of such questions, see P. Keifert, "Mind Reader and Maestro: Models for Understanding the Biblical Interpreter," *Word and World* 1 (1981), 153–68.

5. W. D. Davies, *The Setting of the Sermon on the Mount* (Cambridge: Cambridge Univ. Press, 1966).

6. R. Brown, *The Gospel according to John,* Anchor Bible, 2 vols. (Garden City, N.Y.: Doubleday, 1966–70); J. L. Martyn, *History and Theology in the Fourth Gospel,* rev. ed. (Nashville: Abingdon, 1979).

7. H. Conzelmann, *The Theology of St. Luke,* trans. G. Buswell (London: Faber and Faber, 1960; reprint, Philadelphia: Fortress Press, 1982), and *Acts,* Hermeneia (Philadelphia: Fortress Press, 1989); E. Haenchen, *The Acts of the Apostles* (Philadelphia: Westminster Press, 1971); J. Jervell, *Luke and the People of God* (Minneapolis: Augsburg Books, 1972), and *The Unknown Paul* (Minneapolis: Augsburg Books, 1984).

While reconstructing the communities for which the evangelists wrote is an essential aspect of interpretation, difficulties have developed with the scholarly tradition. The first is the lack of hard data for making historical decisions. We have little archaeological data by which to check proposals about the nature of religious communities in Syria or Asia Minor in the first century of this era. The comparative literary evidence for these decisions, too, is scant. The drastic revision of first century Judaism that has occurred through the finding of some scrolls in caves along the shore of the Dead Sea and some manuscripts buried in an old monastic cemetery in Egypt only indicates how vulnerable we are to historical accidents—and how dependent we are on such historical evidence for hard data.

And if we have little solid information about history external to the Christian movement, we are likewise unclear about much of its internal history. Old scholarly convictions about the rapid Hellenization of the Christian movement—which meant its distancing from Jewish roots— have been seriously called into question.[8] New histories of the first century are being written, and with the recent release of new information from the caves at Qumran we can expect more surprises.

There is no alternative to historical reconstruction, but we must understand its place in the interpretive enterprise. It is not the most stabilizing element in interpretation, particularly when it comes to reconstructing the communities within which the Gospels were read.

Recent scholarship is more sophisticated in this regard. Howard Kee's book on the Markan Community and Vernon Robbins's work on the social setting of Markan rhetoric explore the interrelationship of language and social structure in a way that is less dependent upon precise historical location of the Gospel than on profiling the social setting it presumes.[9] Kee draws on the work of Brian Wilson, Robbins on the work of Clifford Gaertz and Kenneth Burke.[10] Both feel obliged to

8. One of the most vigorous advocates of a new assessment of Jewish Christianity and its place within the first century is Jacob Jervell. His *Luke and the People of God* and *The Unknown Paul* have resulted in a dramatic shift in Lukan scholarship in England and the United States. Hengel's study on *Judaism and Hellenism* (trans. J. Bowden; Philadelphia: Fortress Press, 1974) has borne fruit in the variety of studies done on hellenized Judaism. Classics and Near Eastern studies are far less distant in most New Testament circles than they once were.

9. Howard Clark Kee, *Community of the New Age* (Philadelphia: Westminster Press, 1977); Vernon Robbins, *Jesus the Teacher* (Philadelphia: Fortress Press, 1984). The nature of Kee's analysis does not prevent him, however, from hazarding a guess as to the precise geographical area from which Mark's Gospel derives.

10. Kee, *Community*, p. 177, makes use of Hirsch, *Validity in Interpretation* (New Haven, Conn.: Yale Univ. Press, 1967) to justify his historical work as providing the

demonstrate that the communities they profile are historically conceiv-able, but they do not rely exclusively or even primarily on historical data. We can construct the symbolic universe of religious groups, they argue, from which we may draw some tentative conclusions about their composition, based on analogies from our study of other religious groups. The construct may be tested against the modest information we possess from antiquity and by continued study of religious groups. While we may not know precisely where Mark wrote and for what particular geographical community, we can infer something about the readership by observing its symbolic universe within the larger world of the first century to the degree that its literary traditions may be reconstructed. The larger social and literary construct may serve as one means of evaluating proposals about what the Gospel means.

The Implied Reader

The last decades have witnessed a basic shift in paradigms in biblical studies. Patrick Keifert speaks of a shift from an historical paradigm to a linguistic.[11] At all levels, literary study is displacing historical approaches as the primary mode of interpretation. Scholars regularly speak of attending to the world in front of the text rather than the world behind the text.[12] The shift has resulted in dramatically different assessments of the Gospels and Acts. A major reason is that more than a

---

"general horizon of meaning" against which background the author's intention is to be measured:

> The sage words of E. D. Hirsch with which we began will serve us well as an enduring standard of method, even though no attempt at historical reconstruction may achieve the goal fully: "It is of the utmost importance to determine the horizon which defines the author's intention as a whole, for it is only with reference to this horizon, or sense of the whole, that the interpreter (or historian) may distinguish those implications which are typical and proper components of the meaning from those which are not." The present work represents both an essay in the use of a holistic approach to Mark and an appeal to others to explore the possibilities of a similar method in the historical analysis of primitive Christianity.

Brian Wilson, *Magic and Millennium* (London, 1973) and Max Weber's *Sociology of Religion* provide the logic of his sociological arguments by which he sketches a profile of the Markan "sect."

Robbins, *Jesus,* p. 5–6, employs in his study of literature and culture the work of Kenneth Burke (*Counter-Statement; A Rhetoric of Motives;* and *Language as Symbolic Action*) and Clifford Gaertz (*The Interpretation of Cultures*).

11. Patrick Keifert, "Mind-Reader and Maestro," and "Meaning and Reference: The Interpretation of Verisimilitude in the Gospel according to Mark" (Ph.D. diss., University of Chicago, 1982).

12. We need not understand the statement in naive fashion, as if readers were ever

generation of form critics were trained in such a way as to make their appreciation of a story exceptionally difficult. Thus within biblical scholarship, basic literary skills seem extraordinary and have been received with enthusiasm.

Audience is one element in the experience of any piece of literature.[13] We read a book, naively assuming it was written for us. Or we may read it as outsiders, perhaps because the work presumes much that we do not know or because it is simply difficult to understand. Such experiences of strangeness can lead in different directions. They can alienate or entice. We would define a story as good when it lays hold of readers, not letting them go, forcing them to work hard to make sense—even when sense is unclear.[14] In such cases, of course, it may prove difficult to argue that a particular interpretation is more correct than another— or that one reading is "true."

One reason a literary understanding of audience holds more promise than a historical one is that a story does more than simply presume a readership; it forms one. There is something fictional about all audiences, as Walter Ong rightly points out:

> The present reflections have focused on written fictional narrative as a kind of paradigm for the fictionalizing of writers' "audiences" or readers. But what has been said about fictional narrative applies ceteris paribus to all writing . . . the writer's audience is always a fiction. The historian, the scholar or scientist, and the simple letter writer all fictionalize their audiences, casting them in a made-up role and calling on them to play the role assigned.[15]

This is what rhetoricians call creating an audience. It is necessary in any act of communication, and it is done for rhetorical reasons. Particularly in the case of the Bible, an audience is addressed not simply to affirm what already exists but to create something new—to shape,

---

capable of disengaging themselves from their present contexts, or as if historical constructs had no impact on how works of literature are heard. The statement should be taken to mean that the first and last task of interpreters must be to attend to the material at hand. In a field where distractions are available at every turn, such a simple-minded caution may be warranted.

13. Two of the standard works in thinking about audience are Seymour Chatman, *Story and Discourse: Narrative Structure in Fiction and Film* (Ithaca: Cornell Univ. Press, 1978), and Wayne Booth, *The Rhetoric of Fiction,* 2d. ed. (Chicago: Univ. of Chicago Press, 1983).

14. This is precisely how Mark's Gospel works on readers, as Frank Kermode argues in *Genesis of Secrecy.*

15. Howard Ong, "The Writer's Audience Is Always a Fiction," *Publications of the Modern Language Association of America* 90–91 (1975): [9–21], 18.

change, perhaps even convert readers of a letter or narrative to form a new community.

While such a process is recognized to some extent by those who speak of the Markan community, the analysis of audience is seldom pursued so as to open the contemporary reader to such persuasion within the Bible. Historical study creates distances that both afford protection and make the experience of reading something less than transforming.

The fictional audience is important to the successful reading of a work. Wayne Booth describes the interplay between author and audience in this fashion:

> The implied author of each novel is someone with whose beliefs on all subjects I must largely agree if I am to enjoy his work. . . . Regardless of my real beliefs and practices, I must subordinate my mind and heart to the book if I am to enjoy it to the full. The author creates, in short, an image of himself and another image of his reader; he makes his reader, as he makes his second self, and the most successful reading is one in which the created selves, author and reader, can find complete agreement.[16]

How do we construct an image of this implied reader? Or to put the question another way, how might analysis of this implied reader critique our own experience as an audience? If historical reconstruction may serve as a way of opening new horizons or providing constraint on our reading, at least as much may be expected of literary analysis.

What are readers expected to know? At the most elementary level, Mark's readers are expected to know Greek. If we do not speak the language, we will require translations. And readers are supposed to recognize that Jesus did not speak Greek. While they may not know Aramaic and require translation of the few phrases Mark uses (5:41; 7:34; 14:36; 15:34), they are at least to recognize that Jesus was a stranger in important ways. He did not speak the language of the audience—even Mark's original audience! This distance is preserved even in English translation, where Greek is translated but the Aramaic only transliterated. The mere employment of Aramaic phrases suggests that those who believe authors intend readers to identify with characters in their stories do not understand the complexity of the relationship between story and reader. Mark's readers are not part of Jesus' world in many respects, and that sense of distance is an important element in the working of the story.

On the other hand, readers are expected to know certain facts. They are expected to know what it means that something is written in Isaiah

16. Booth, *Rhetoric of Fiction*, 137–38.

the prophet;[17] they are presumed to know something about John the Baptist. While we may not be able to locate the readership in a precise location and a precise time, we can suggest something about the sort of audience the narrative implies and creates.[18]

There are several advantages in examining an implied audience—the audience the text rhetorically constructs—prior to asking historical questions. One's point of departure is the text itself which, while hardly without ambiguity, is at least more stable than historical constructs that change with every new discovery—constructs for which, in many instances, the text is one of the few sources. More importantly, the connection between an implied reader and actual readers today is more easily established than a connection between ourselves and a mythic historical construct. If the task of interpretation is to engage our contemporaries in a new reading of the story, emphasis on the world of the story—whether constructing its symbolic universe, its implied author, or implied audience—offers far greater promise of accomplishing such engagement than mere historical reconstruction.

The role of historical work is to help fill in what the story presumes we know so that we can make sense of it, to open our imaginations to experiences beyond our own, and to provide a way of testing interpretations. The argument I will make that Mark's implied audience is scripturally literate will be considerably strengthened if we can show that a large Greek-speaking Jewish community existed long before Christianity made its appearance, a community that read its Bible in Greek, established interpretive traditions on the basis of the Greek text, and had constructed a symbolic universe in conversation with their Greek as well as their Jewish heritage. Few today would deny that such a Jewish community existed. That it existed has immense ramifications for our understanding of the implied audience—and it is precisely this understanding that shapes the expectations of our own interpretive community.

Mark's Implied Audience

What sort of readership does the Gospel presume and what kind of community does it seek to create? While the first task must be attention

17. That the citation is not simply from Isaiah the prophet may raise interesting questions about the implied author's grasp of the biblical tradition. The citation may be studied for the light it can shed on the history of early Christian interpretive tradition as well.

18. This is also the intention of Robbins in his socio-rhetorical analysis of the hellenistic world of which Mark and the Markan audience were a part.

to the rhetorical features of the narrative argument—how the Gospel works its audience—the second task will be to take seriously the constraints of historical context. Proposed readings of Mark that cannot be squared with historical study must be regarded as unconvincing.[19] Study of the first Markan Community is important to the degree that it shapes the expectations of the present readership and serves as a constraint on imaginative proposals.[20] I am grateful for the opportunity to make explicit arguments for a Markan audience that is presumed by my commentary on Mark. I seek to shape it as one engaged in the rhetorical enterprise we call exegesis.

The Markan Community in which I am interested is the community that will be persuaded that the Gospel deserves a hearing and whose imaginations will be engaged and moved by the narrative. What are the obstacles to such engagement? One may be simply the lack of a practiced imagination. A large majority of readers expect little from their encounter with the Bible. They have had scant opportunity to be attentive to large blocks of narrative. Reading of the Bible has been piecemeal, often in church where it is poorly executed. Such readers need to experience the possibilities of narratives.[21]

19. In this regard I very much agree with Kee and Robbins in their insistence on establishing the historical context within which the Gospel should be read. It should likewise be clear that I do not agree with the radical separation of reader-oriented criticism and historical study advocated by Tolbert (*Sowing the Gospel*, 57):

> If the Gospels are to continue as *living* texts, then modern readers must always be able to interpret them in the light of current theological reflection and discourse. The terms used to describe the new or unique character of the Gospels by scholars (e.g., kerygma, parable) are not "new" or "unique" to their own peers and thus are suitable designations for the shared generic expectations of current readers. Those scholars who have explored the Greco-Roman and Jewish milieu of the Gospels, on the other hand, while still contemporary interpreters themselves, are attempting to read the Gospels in the light of their *authorial audience*. Thus the division between the two major streams of research on the gospel genre may be understood as attempts to clarify the reading process in terms of quite different, but equally legitimate, audiences, the contemporary and the authorial.

20. In this regard, Harvey's *Jesus and the Constraints of History* (Philadelphia: Westminster, 1982) serves a useful purpose in Gospel criticism, both in terms of his formal approach as well as his concrete proposals. His priorities, however—beginning with historical reconstruction as a context for reading specific texts—seem reversed.

21. In this regard Robert Tannehill's experiment with commentary form in his two-volume work on Luke-Acts deserves attention: *The Narrative Unity of Luke-Acts: A Literary Interpretation* (Philadelphia and Minneapolis: Fortress Press, 1986, 1990). His commentary is largely an exploration of the argument in Luke's two-part work, for which various interpretive approaches are enlisted in an engagement with the "world in front of the text."

Another obstacle is the cultural distance between our age and that of the time of the Bible. Cross-cultural reading requires a willingness to encounter people not exactly like us—so that we may eventually glimpse a broader and richer human experience that determines new horizons of meaning. While we can never pretend to know the Markan Community of the first century, historical reconstruction can make us more knowledgeable and perceptive readers. Of the features of the implied audience that might be examined, I have selected two: the relationship of the audience to Jewish tradition, and the location of the audience in the world.

The People of God

The audience Mark's Gospel addresses is to view itself as the people of God, a term located firmly in Israel's heritage. As the people of God, a certain kind of knowledge, a certain relationship to the tradition is presupposed. By attending to Mark's rhetoric we can sketch the contours of this knowledge and relationship to the tradition.

Scriptural Knowledge

First of all, Mark's audience has a knowledge of the Scriptures.[22] Explicit quotations introduced by formulas include: 1:2-3 (Isaiah the prophet); 7:6-7 (Isa. 29:13); 7:10 (Exod. or Deut.); 10:6-8 (Gen. 2:24); 11:17 (Isa. 56:7; Jer. 7:11); 12:10-11 (Ps. 118:22); 12:19 (Gen. 38:8); 12:26 (Exod. 3:1,6,15); 12:29-30 (Deut. 6:5; Lev. 19:18); 12:36 (Ps. 110:1); 14:27 (Zech. 13:7).

The depth of scriptural knowledge is perhaps even more apparent when we consider allusions to biblical passages not marked with a formula. It is a more difficult question, of course, to ask what words the narrative expects an audience to recognize as scriptural when introductory formulas are absent. One might argue that certain narratives were born from scriptural seeds the kernel of which has long been forgotten by the time the material is recorded in the Gospel. There are places, however, where the scriptural allusions play an important role in the narrative: They make a difference in how the reality being described is to be understood. This is particularly true in the passion story.

---

22. The term *graphe* is used three times in Mark (12:10,24; 14:49); forms of the verb *graphein* appear ten times in the technical sense. Absent are other technical terms, like those found in Matthew and Luke: *nomos* never appears; "prophet" in an introduction of a scriptural citation appears only once.

Among the passages where scriptural allusions are recognizable I would include 14:62 (Dan. 7:13; Ps. 110:1); 15:24 (Ps. 22:19), 15:29 (Ps. 22:8), 15:34 (Ps. 22:2), and 15:36 (Ps. 69:22). Crucial in each case are the words of the biblical passages themselves.

First, Jesus' only words at his trial before the Jewish court (14:62) are taken from the Scriptures, in particular Psalm 110:1 and Daniel 7:13 (Perrin argued for Zechariah 10:12 as well).[23] The appearance of Psalm 110:1 in an explicit citation earlier in the Gospel (12:36) makes it likely that readers are expected to recognize the words in 14:62 as scriptural. One can make the argument based on a study of the two scriptural passages in earlier Christian tradition as well.[24] It is significant that Jesus, who "goes as it is written of him" (14:21; cf. 9:12), uses some of the scriptural words in promising vindication over against his judges, words taken from texts that by Mark's day had a significant place in Christian tradition.

The prominence of Psalm 22 in the passion story is likewise difficult to ignore for those with even a passing knowledge of the Scriptures. While an argument may be offered about the place of the psalm in the development of the passion story, its repeated occurrence—particularly in Jesus' last words—presumes some awareness on the part of the audience that what is taking place has "been written." The lack of citation formulas gives evidence of a kind of narrative scriptural argument rather than scriptural proof (more common in the setting of controversies).

The offer of vinegar to Jesus in 15:36 may be an allusion to Psalm 69:21. That an implied audience is expected to recognize the scriptural language can be argued from the prominence of scriptural language earlier in the story, the importance of these particular biblical passages in the history of Christian tradition, and their utility in contributing to the ironic tone of the narrative. A proper appreciation of the "reality" being narrated involves recognizing a dimension of truth obscured from the participants in the story. Jesus' death as King is according to the Scriptures. The irony—an experience of the distance between the way things appear and the way they really are—is enhanced by the employment of scriptural allusions (however their presence in the story may be explained in genetic terms).

The audience of the Gospel is expected, however, not only to know about the Scriptures as a general phenomenon and in particular, but to

23. N. Perrin, "Mark 14:62: The End Product of a Christian Pesher Tradition?" NTS 12 (1966): 150–55.

24. See Juel, *Messianic Exegesis* and Hay, *Glory at the Right Hand*, SBLDS 18 (Nashville: Abingdon, 1973).

know something about their employment. Several instances feature careful scriptural interpretation in the narrative. Three of the most striking occur in the context of controversies. The first is Mark 7:1-13. The extended controversy arises from a criticism by "the Pharisees and some of the scribes who had come from Jerusalem" that Jesus' disciples do not observe "the tradition of the elders" (a technical term for the Oral Law, as is clear from later rabbinic tradition). Interpreters have made much of the explanation offered to Mark's audience about the practices of "the Pharisees, and all the Jews," who wash their hands before they eat. Most often, the remarks are taken as evidence of an audience with little sympathy for Jewish dietary laws. The elaborate story, however, like the earlier controversies, presumes a readership with much invested in Israel's law as it was lived among contemporaries. The thoroughly Jewish character of the argument that follows is often overlooked.[25] A scriptural denunciation of a particular Pharisaic practice is based on an interpretation of Exodus 20 (or Deuteronomy 5). The general denunciation of "this people" in Isaiah 29:13 is focused on Pharisees whose practice of dedicating property as "korban" is characterized as a violation of the commandment to honor one's parents. Such interpretation certainly belongs within the realm of school argument. The extended discussion of clean and unclean, concluding with the striking "thus he declared all foods clean" (7:19), presumes a knowledge of tradition, Scriptures, and the character of legal argument. If the readership needs clarification about some Pharisaic practices, it is nevertheless expected to know how scriptural argument is carried out and what investment it has in scriptural precedent for its actions.

A second example of scriptural interpretation is found in Mark 12:18-27. The discussion with the Sadducees presumes an awareness of controversy within the Jewish community about the resurrection, a knowledge of scriptural arguments against the doctrine, and an appreciation of scriptural arguments on behalf of the notion of resurrection. The Sadducean citation of Deuteronomy 25 and Genesis 38—rules regarding Levirite marriage—renders some understandings of the resurrection absurd, at least in their view. God's law would never have allowed for such complications had it the resurrection in view. In Jesus' response, the citation of Exodus 6 corresponds almost exactly with rabbinic arguments for the resurrection from the Torah. The proof here is the

---

25. Cf. Martin Hengel's article "Mc 7,3 *pugme:* Die Geschichte einer exegetischen Aporie und der Versuch ihrer Lösung," ZNW 60 (1969): 182–98. Hengel suggests that the word "fist" is a technical term, thus presuming intimate knowledge of the legal discussions about washing.

absence of the past tense of the verb, "was." If God *is* the God of Abraham, Isaac, and Jacob, there must be a resurrection, since "he is God not of the dead, but of the living" (Mark 12:27).

Finally, there is the striking argument about the Christ as David's son in 12:35-37.[26] The failure of most interpreters to understand the argument of the passage relates directly to the lack in understanding the logic of scriptural argument. The passage provides a good example of exploiting an alleged contradiction in the Scriptures to one's advantage. Knowledge of standard messianic promises is presumed (esp. 2 Sam. 7:10-14; Isa. 11:1; Zech. 6:12; Jer. 23:5-6; 33:14-18) according to which the promised deliverer—the Christ—is from the line of David.[27] The employment of Psalm 110:1 as an argument for the Christ's status as lord presumes that the passage was generally regarded as messianic among Jewish readers; it also presumes Christian interpretation of the biblical passage as an explication of Jesus' resurrection. The apparent contradiction between 2 Samuel 7:12 and Psalm 110:1 is overcome only if the messianic candidate is enthroned at God's right hand (in Christian terms, only if the risen Jesus is also the Christ). Only in this case it is appropriate for David (the prophet) to refer to his son as lord. The argumentation is as technical and as intricate as any in the New Testament.

Inside Knowledge

In addition to knowledge of the Scriptures of Israel, Mark's implied audience has access to technical information appropriate to those familiar with the Jewish community. They are alert, for example, to the distinction between the use of the terms "Jew" and "Israel." In the story of Jesus' death, there is a marked difference in the way characters speak. When Jews speak of Jesus' alleged claim to office, they use the expressions "Christ, the Son of the Blessed One" (14:61) and "the Christ, the King of Israel" (15:31). When Romans speak, it is "the King of the Jews" and "God's son."[28] "Jew" was in fact not the preferred self-identification

26. Representative interpretations of this passage are discussed in Evald Loevestam's "Die Davidssohnsfrage," SEA 27 (1972): 72–82. In the essay he argues convincingly the case that I am presenting. See also the comments by Wm. Lane, *The Gospel according to Mark,* NICNT (Grand Rapids: Eerdmans, 1974); and Nils A. Dahl, "Contradictions in Scripture," *Studies in Paul* (Minneapolis: Augsburg Books, 1977), 159–77. For a fuller discussion of the passage, see "The Origins of Mark's Christology," in this volume.

27. See Juel, *Messianic Exegesis,* 59–88.

28. The translation of *huios theou* is a notorious problem. Should the definite article be supplied or not, and should translators write "son" or "Son?" A critical question is

in the Jewish world but was typical of non-Jewish usage. The narrative provides a sense of how the language ought to sound when different characters are speaking.

The difference from John's Gospel is particularly noteworthy, where the phrase "the Jews" is employed by the narrator over 80 times. John's audience is expected to recognize the Jews as an alien group (although even here, "the Christians" is not an alternative label provided by John, and one of Jesus' followers can be called an Israelite [John 1:47]). Only once in Mark is "the Jews" used outside the passion narrative, namely in 7:3, where the narrator's parenthetical comment refers to "the Pharisees and all the Jews." Nowhere else do the Jews appear as a group; nowhere else is there a possibility for Mark's readers to understand themselves as something distinct from Jews.

Another area of familiarity presumed for Mark's readers is the structure of the Jewish community. Mark is the most careful about differentiating its various groups. Except for 7:3 ("The Pharisees and all the Jews"), the only occurrence of "the Jews" is in chapter 15, where Romans identify Jesus five times as "King of the Jews." Otherwise, Mark carefully differentiates between Pharisees, Sadducees, Herodians, and officials (scribes, chief priests, and elders). While there are references to scribes and "scribes of the Pharisees" early in the story, clearly official are the "scribes" who appear with the chief priests and elders as the Temple officials and heads of the Jerusalem government.[29]

Although technical terms like "sect" are not employed, Pharisees appear in the story as people concerned with the tradition of the elders, with food laws, sabbath observance, ritual purity, and taxes. In the one appearance of the Sadducees, they advocate a view of the tradition that leaves no room for a doctrine of the resurrection of the dead. Pharisees, Herodians, and Sadducees thus appear as interest groups, people with a particular point of view about the tradition set off from the rest of the community. They are not confused with the officials (the scribes, chief priests, and elders), and there is no sense in which any one group represents all Israel. There is no attempt to make blanket statements about the Jews or Israel.[30] That also means there is no attempt to draw a world in which "Israel" is a monolithic reality.

---

how the "confession" is to be heard. Most likely the statement of the Centurion should be heard in line with the statements made by other Romans in the narrative: they speak the truth, but in mockery. The past tense, "was," speaks in any case against regarding the Centurion's comment as anything but an evaluation of someone now dead and gone.

29. See Paul Winter, *On the Trial of Jesus* (Berlin: Gruyter, 1961). While Winter's concerns are historical, his observations about usage in Mark represent careful exegesis.

30. The point is made by scholars as different as Étienne Trocmé (*The Formation of the Gospel according to Mark,* trans. P. Gaughan [Philadelphia: Westminster Press, 1973; 1st ed., 1963]) and Paul Winter (*On the Trial of Jesus* [Berlin: Gruyter, 1961]).

Such knowledge of Scripture and the realities of the Jewish community presume an audience with both knowledge of and investments in the traditions of the people of God.

Implied Identity

Given such implied knowledge, how is the Markan audience as projected by the narrative to understand itself in terms of traditional categories? The question is made difficult by the absence of familiar terminology. The term "Christian" is not employed; the closest Mark comes is the phrase "of Christ" in 9:41 ("For truly I tell you, whoever gives you a cup of water because you are of Christ will by no means lose the reward" RSV[31]). Thus, readers are not given the opportunity to understand themselves as Christian as opposed to Jewish. Apart from 7:3-4, the category "Jew" appears only in the account of the passion, where it is used by Romans (King of the Jews). "Israel" occurs only twice, the second occurrence in the phrase "The Christ, the King of Israel" in 15:32.

The first occurrence of "Israel" bears closer scrutiny. In the last of the controversies in chapter 12, in response to a question about the greatest commandment asked by a scribe, Jesus quotes Deuteronomy 6:4-5 (The "Shema"). The command to love God is addressed to Israel. The scribe who asks the question and who approves of Jesus' response—whom Jesus pronounces "not far from the Kingdom of God"—is surely included within Israel. The narrative makes no effort to create distance between readers and the Israel to whom the commandment is addressed.

On the contrary, readers are addressed throughout the Gospel as having an investment in Israel's tradition and Scriptures. They are, because of this investment, to understand the vast distance between traditional expectation and the fulfillment of God's promises, between what passes for doing the will of God and what is actually obedience. The world is portrayed ironically, as characterized by oppositions: There are "human things" and "divine things" (Mark 8:31-33). Yet these oppositions do not lend themselves to translation into categories like "Christian" or "Gentile." Piety is defined by the commandments (7:10 and 12:29-31). Jesus goes "as it has been written of him." Differences are adjudicated by appeal to Israel's Scriptures.

Further, disputes about Jewish matters are not simply allegories depicting some other political or social realities. While the disputes have

---

31. The NRSV's "because you bear the name of Christ" is an unwarranted paraphrase. There is no technical employment of "name" as in Paul or Acts.

social and political dimensions, they have to do with membership in Israel. Sabbath and food laws, taxes to Caesar and worship of the One God are of concern to the audience for whom Mark writes. The story speaks of a Kingdom of God that cannot be contained in old forms: Fresh skins for new wine. It speaks of a presence of God that cannot be domesticated by tradition, but it addresses a group that must understand itself within the framework of God's dealings with Israel. The God who raised Jesus from the dead is no stranger, but the one who called Abraham and Isaac, the one who spoke through the prophets, the one whose promises can be trusted. While the theological argument is subtle, everything depends upon the fidelity of the One in whose hands the future lies. The truth of the story depends on things yet to come. That is the point of chapter 13. Yet the narrative must convince that there is reason to await expectantly the return of the Son of Man on the clouds, when "all will see."

To that extent, the identity of the readership as the people of God is crucial, even if the expression is never employed. The absence of such traditional religious language, particularly in comparison with the works of Matthew, Luke, and John, indicates not so much early Hellenization as a situation in which the real crisis within the Jewish community still lies in the future. While there is surely controversy about Jesus' place within Israel's tradition, there is no sense that Jesus' resurrection marks the end of Israel and the beginning of something new.[32] It marks the end of the Temple, perhaps, and radical changes in appreciating the heritage, but there is yet no divide between Christian and Jew. The radical increase in the use of such expression as "the Jews" in John and Acts marks a new stage in the crisis within Israel—not yet a radical break (even in John, "Christian" is not a category) but certainly a step closer to that break.

The Community and "The World"

I must be more brief here. My comments are more suggestive than exhaustive. I have argued above that to identify the Markan audience

---

32. Compare this view with that of Howard Kee (*Community of the New Age,* 114–15), which is typical of commentators:

> Similarly, for Mark the incident of the withered fig tree (Mark 11:12-14) is not a miracle story but an allegory of the curse on faithless Israel. The lesson to be drawn from it is less of a polemic against the old covenant people than a warning to the new covenant people (11:20-25).

Trocmé, representing a minority opinion, advocates the opposite conclusion in *Formation,* p. 207: "Thus the Christian mission is marching on, not towards the constitution of another chosen people but towards the eschatological restoration of Israel . . ."

as Christian or Gentile does not do justice to the narrative. No such simple labels are provided. Nor does the narrative create a sense of being a church in the way Paul's letters do, with identifiable social structures and networks. There are some such indicators, but they are not nearly as easily ferreted out as in the case of the other Gospels.

Family imagery is one way to speak about following Jesus. "Whoever does the will of God is my brother and sister and mother," Jesus says (Mark 3:35); he explicitly promises that those who leave "house or brothers or sisters or mother or father or children or fields, for my sake and for the sake of the good news" will receive "a hundredfold now in this age—houses, brothers and sisters, and mothers and children, and fields with persecutions" (10:29-30).[33] The world is not a place where the faithful will be comfortable, but it is also not a place where they will be alone.

The narrative takes pains to shape that world in which the faithful will live. Standards will be turned on their heads: the last will be first (10:31); men and women must become like children; leaders must become like servants and slaves (9:33-36; 10:41-45). The world in which believers must live can be depicted only by means of irony. Things are not as they appear—to the simple, the allegedly important, even to the faithful. There is a tension between "divine things" and "human things" (8:33), somehow related to the relationship between God and Satan. But there is no absolute chasm between appearance and reality. The world to which the reader is invited is the same world in which the reader lives, a world that is the suitable arena for the work of God and the faithful.[34]

Mark's vision of the world is ironic. But an ironic vision can function in more than one way for an audience. It may serve as a word of encouragement for those whose vision is not shared by the majority and those whose opinions matter. It has been typical in Markan scholarship to understand the audience as outsiders—persecuted members

33. Tannehill in *The Sword of His Mouth: Forceful and Imaginative Language in Synoptic Sayings,* Semeia Supplements 1 (Philadelphia: Fortress Press, 1975), 147–52, argues that the "with persecutions" makes the whole statement ironic. That is perhaps true, but there is little reason to discount the promise of a new community in this age.

34. Vernon Robbins nicely describes the setting within which rhetoric operates in *Jesus the Teacher,* 6–7: "Opponents can join battle only through a mediatory ground that makes communication possible. . . . The mediatory ground is constituted by a 'general body of identifications that owe their convincingness much more to trivial repetition and dull daily reenforcement than to exceptional skills.'" "Newness," "surprise," "scandal," and "irony" presume shared ground. Readers have an investment in that shared ground. If they had not, Jesus' story could not be told at all. Because it can be communicated through narrative, there must be some link with the world in which we all live.

of Roman society desperately in need of encouragement in the face of impending death. While Jesus' initial invitation to "take up their cross and follow me" may hold out the prospect of death (8:34-35), martyrdom is not a pervasive theme in Mark. And there is little evidence that the Gospel struggles with the problem of social and political location within Roman society, which accords well with our understanding of the history of the first century. The place of Christians within the Empire becomes a major problem only in the second century. Jewish concerns seem far more central. And as I believe a study of Mark 13 demonstrates, encouragement does not aptly characterize the address to the implied reader.[35] The image of wakefulness in the little parable that concludes chapter 13 suggests an implied reader—a reader who is directly addressed ("What I say to you I say to all")—whose greatest danger is falling asleep. There are those within the household who have been given authority by the master of the house and tasks to perform (13:34). The question is whether they will be found about their business when the master returns—or will be found asleep. While the irony may be employed for comfort and consolation, it may as well serve as warning and promise.

"Keep awake" is quite different from "Remain steadfast." The problem on which the narrative invests most of its energy—the inability of the disciples to grasp the "mystery of the Kingdom" entrusted to them—is brought to bear on the problem of overconfidence. Even insiders are not in touch with "divine things"; they are utterly unprepared for the crises that lie ahead, both within the story world and beyond it. They fall asleep, perhaps with dreams of the kingdom in which they will have places of honor. They have no sense of what it will mean to take a place at Jesus' right and left, at least in this age. There are signs for those who know where to look; there are promises for those who cannot remain steadfast. But insiders need to know where to look for help, and where false hopes lie in wait.

The Markan Community in the sense of an implied audience makes most sense as one in which the world has proved more hospitable than anticipated. Institutional language appropriate to a structured community is employed to speak about relations among the faithful. The disciples are instructed in how to exercise authority (10:33-45). While they are not to impose their authority as the Gentiles, they are expected to exercise it properly. When the master of the house leaves, he gives authority to his slaves and assigns tasks for them to perform (13:34). The faithful need to be warned about the abuse of authority among the

35. See "Watching in Spite of Weariness," chap. 6 in this volume.

Gentiles, about false prophets and Christs, about the trials and tests that lie ahead. The temptation to self-confidence is always present. Confidence in one's ability to see and hear can be as effective a barrier to the grace of God as the tradition of the elders. The implied reader is offered a glimpse of how things are; the future holds dangers and trials. God's presence in coming events will offer surprises both more disquieting and more promising than even the elect can have imagined. Readers are invited to "Keep Awake."

It is not a small matter that the truth with which the implied audience is confronted is finally a public truth. The Gospel does not seek to create an elect isolated from the world. There is a sense, to be sure, that truth is not achievable as an ordinary human enterprise; to be grasped by the surprising grace of God is something akin to the blind receiving sight or the dead coming to life. The confrontation with "divine things" involves a necessary stripping away of the veil. The struggle between God's ways and those of this age will continue as long as there is breath, and the lack of closure in the story indicates that the distance between the two realities has not been overcome in a final sense. But the promises of God are not only for an elect who somehow grasp what others cannot. "All will see." The truth of the Gospel is finally a public one that can be proclaimed; it lends itself to narrative argument. Mark's implied audience, ultimately, is all the world. The rhetoric of the Gospel generates testimony and mission, never escape.

Implications for a Contemporary Rhetorical Strategy

It should be clear to most within the academy that interpreters have succeeded in creating a scholarly audience interested in an historical description of early Christianity. Any proposed interpretation must be able to make its case historically. It is thus quite appropriate to ask if the implied reader profiled here is conceivable historically. I believe the profile fits better than other sketches an emerging portrait of early Christianity. For the audience to which Mark writes, Jewish matters have not been left far behind in the process of Hellenization, the delay of the Parousia is not the principal crisis that precipitated the writing of the Gospels, and early Christianity was not a massive experience of failure. It would undoubtedly be helpful to say more about this historical community. What did it look like? How did people live? What were the structures of their corporate life? How did they relate to the world?

Such questions deserve further scrutiny as we explore what the Gospel means in all its dimensions.

Most important to my mind is the grasping of a rhetorical agenda by which we are made aware of what is involved in becoming an audience for the Gospel's theological arguments. Of primary significance are the arguments the narrative makes for contemporary readers—arguments about the nature of our experience of God and the world, arguments that can result in the building of a new Markan community. Two features of Mark's rhetorical construct of an implied audience stand out.

We might term the first an awareness of being the people of God, that is, Abraham's heirs; the second is having a place in the world, some access to the public, and some genuine power. I highlight these two features of the implied audience because, according to most commentators, Mark writes for Gentiles with little interest in Jewish matters, and for a marginalized church with little prospect other than persecution and martyrdom. Both these views, I have argued, are incorrect, and the views have important implications for our own hearing of the Gospel.

Mark's Readers and the People of God

Who are the groups for whom Mark writes? They have an investment in Israel's Scriptures. They are concerned enough about sabbath observance and purity laws to remember Jesus' pronouncements about such matters to justify radical practices. Some of the views they are expected to accept are little different from Pharisaic-type Jews who knew of the Temple's destruction. That Jesus is the Messiah must be explicated as a key to understanding how it is with us and God. If these things are true, how can we take any other view than that Mark's audience is to understand itself as the people of God? And because Mark is careful to tie the impending destruction of Jerusalem to the rejection of Jesus by the Temple leaders, there is no justification for speaking about a new people of God or a new Israel.

The people of God issue has significant theological implications. It is, after all, the God of Abraham, Isaac, and Jacob who raised Jesus from the dead, vindicating the crucified Messiah. What does that event suggest about a reading of Israel's heritage? The matters are dealt with much more explicitly in Matthew, Luke, and John—perhaps because the questions had become unavoidable in the tense decades after the destruction of the Temple. If Mark predates such a struggle, there is little to suggest that his is a Pauline Gospel intended for Gentiles. Even Paul must deal with the whole matter of Israel and unbelief. Mark presumes an audience that locates itself in Israel's heritage.

What does this location within Israel's heritage mean for the Markan audience in the present? If contemporary Christian readers of Mark do not so locate themselves—if we have never understood the law as the mark of God's chosen and have, in fact, simply appropriated the whole notion of election as something applying directly to us—the distance between our own situation and that of the implied audience cries for attention. The Marcionite solution of the problem may preserve the sense of surprise and irony in Mark, but the irony is of a different sort than Mark's, and the abandonment of Israel's heritage shifts the move from mission to escape, from world-affirming to world-denying—precisely because the God whom the Marcionites believe to be disclosed in the narrative is alien, a being other than Israel's God.

It is an understatement that the nexus of issues identified by the theme "the people of God" requires further attention. A profile of Mark's implied audience demands that current readers not only do some home-work but undertake a new assay of theological investments in Jewish matters regarded as passé since perhaps the second century. Mark's Gospel, as the rest of the writings in the New Testament, can be read as promising only if the God who plays such a major role in the story can be trusted. If God does not keep promises to Israel, there is little reason for Gentiles to expect anything. Reading Mark's story as promising means understanding the investments that bind the Christian movement tightly to its Jewish ancestry.

Mark's Readers and the World

A gnosticizing reading of Mark is a constant temptation. The implied audience, according to conventional wisdom, is a threatened group with few prospects in the world. The Gospel serves as a promise of future salvation. The categorizing of Mark as "apocalyptic" only serves to further such a view: Mark's community, like other sects, remains on the fringes of society with little hope of building a new world. Jesus is the prophet who challenges the society, and dies for it. The future will bring vindication; the present is a time for faithful endurance.

Read from an apocalyptic perspective, it is not surprising that Mark's Gospel creates an audience further distanced from the world and its institutions, feeding off persecution, dealing with suffering by labeling it a virtue, finding little impetus for mission or for service in the world.

This is why an accurate profiling of the implied audience is crucial. From the outset, readers know what the disciples and all the participants cannot. They are fed with promises throughout the Gospel, some of which are fulfilled, others of which point to the future beyond the story time. The problem to which the narrative opens readers is not simply persecution. The disciples are offered the prospect of genuine power and authority. They are instructed in how not to employ authority and position (10:42-45), implying that some will exercise authority in the community of the faithful. In the little parable concluding chapter 13, the word "authority" appears again: The (new) master of the house grants authority and assigns tasks within his household. (See also the parable about binding the strong man and despoiling his house in 3:27.) The gospel will be preached to all the nations (13:10). The time of openness will come. There will be a "new temple not made with hands" in which the implied audience will have a place and a role to play.

Interestingly, many of the problems about which Jesus warns his followers ("you . . . [and] all" in 13:37) relate not to persecutions from the outside world but to internal conflicts: family disintegration, false claims, and false leaders (13:6, 12-13, 21-22). The disciples already struggle over position, concerned about "who is the greatest" and who will get to sit at Jesus' right and left hand (9:33-37; 10:35-45). Such problems engage present readers in a manner quite differently from those associated with a persecuted and desperate religious minority.

The surprise ending of the Gospel is intended for the implied audience. Its impact does not easily fit the image of an implied audience desperate and in need of comfort. The conclusion offers little comfort. The impact of the ending has more to do with expectations of satisfaction and control. Readers have been treated as insiders throughout the story, learning what none of the characters can know. It is not difficult to imagine an ending to the story that would reinforce that experience, providing readers with a sense of closure and satisfaction at the expense of the disciples. Yet the empty tomb and the silent women do not provide such satisfaction for those who have been led to expect such an ending, and the events do not leave resolution of the story in the hands of readers. There is something disquieting about that lack of control—a disquiet that usually drives interpreters to get what they need from the story by means of cunning or violence.

The surprise, the irony, work differently if directed at insiders whose problem is indifference or a tired lack of perception about the way things are. It may serve as a warning, as Paul's reminders do in the opening chapters of his first letter to the Corinthians. The features of his message that initially moved the Corinthians from darkness to light, identifying the change that came at their conversion, now serve to illumine their Christian piety, which turns out to have much in common with their pagan past.

Viewing the audience as tired or indifferent is appropriate to the present situation of most Christians, weary of waiting, tempted to believe that the master of the house will never return, increasingly comfortable in a world capable of hiding from the truth, unaware of how easily the authority of the gospel is exchanged for ordinary power.

Careful attention to the implied audience in Mark's story of Jesus may serve to remove barriers to a fruitful hearing of the Gospel for those whose problem is not persecution as much as an inability to be surprised by the God who is both more dangerous and more promising than they can have imagined.

Index of Ancient and Modern Authors

Index of Ancient Sources